Create
Space

To my mothers, for making the right decision.

DK LONDON
Senior Acquisitions Editor Stephanie Milner
Managing Art Editor Bess Daly
Editor Krissy Mallett
Design and Art Direction StudioROY
Production Editor David Almond
Production Controller Stephanie McConnell

First published in Great Britain in 2021 by
Dorling Kindersley Limited
DK, One Embassy Gardens, 8 Viaduct Gardens,
London, SW11 7BW

Artwork copyright © Thomas Hedger, 2021
Portrait photography copyright © Zoe Timmers, 2021

A CIP catalogue record for this book
is available from the British Library.
ISBN: 978-0-2414-7928-5

Printed and bound in Latvia

For the curious
www.dk.com

This book was made with Forest
Stewardship Council ™ certified
paper – one small step in DK's
commitment to a sustainable future.
For more information go to
www.dk.com/our-green-pledge

Dilly Carter

Declutter Dollies

Create Space

Declutter Your Home
To Clear Your Mind

Chaos

8   The Trail of Destruction
10   Hello, I'm Dilly Carter
14   Reclaim Your Space
19   A Tale of Chaos to Calm
20   Reclaim Your Headspace 101

Bedroom

26   Make Your Bedroom Your Sanctuary
28   Surprising Things That Might Affect Your Sleep
30   Shop Smarter and Question Your Fashion Buys
34   How to Arrange a Feel-good Wardrobe
41   Packing 101
42   Dolly Dash
44   Bedroom Checklist

Bathroom

50   Have a Vision for the Bathroom
52   Edit Your Products
54   How to Clean Up Your Bathroom
56   Dolly Dash
57   Bathroom Checklist

Kitchen

62   Create a Kitchen That Flows
64   A Tale of Chaos to Calm
66   Use Containers to Control Your Spending
68   Organize Your Fridge and Freezer
70   Reduce Your Counter Clutter
72   How to Organize Your Kitchen
75   Zoning Spaces 101
76   Dolly Dash
77   Kitchen Checklist

Utility

82   Create Space with Purpose
84   Sort Out Your Cleaning Products
86   How to Rework Your Utility
87   Love Your Linen 101
88   Dolly Dash
89   Utility Checklist

Dining

94   Clear Up, Dine In, Chill Out
95   Let Go of Perfection 101
96   Don't Save Your Best for Best
98   How to Maximize Storage
100   Dolly Dash
101   Dining Checklist

Living

106 Make a Laid-back Living Space

108 Change Your View, Change Your Mood

110 Heirlooms 101

111 Create Space for Multigenerational Living

112 How to Arrange Books and Records

115 A Tale of Chaos to Calm

116 Dolly Dash

117 Living Checklist

Entrance

122 Make Your First Impression Count

124 Use Your Under-stairs Space

125 Overhaul Your Shoe Storage

126 How to Keep Mail and Keys Under Control

128 Dolly Dash

129 Entrance Checklist

Office

134 Write the 'Job Spec' for Your Space

136 Digitize Your Documents

138 Don't Let Work Affect Your Relationships

140 How to Create the Ultimate Office Space

142 Dolly Dash

143 Office Checklist

Kids

148 Go Back to School

150 Why Are We Attached to Toys?

153 Teach Your Kids Decluttering 101

154 How to Organize Toys

156 Dolly Dash

157 Kids Checklist

Spare Spaces

162 Transform Spare Spaces

164 Blank Space and Structure

166 How to Sort Sentimental Things

168 Dolly Dash

169 Spare Spaces Checklist

Calm

174 Realize Your Vision

176 Create Space

Resources

180 Look After Your Mental Health

182 Donate Responsibly

183 My Favourite Places to Resell and Buy

186 Essential Kit

188 **Index**

191 **Acknowledgements**

192 **Declutter Dollies**

Chaos

The Trail of Destruction

Your alarm clock bleeps, waking you from another terrible night's sleep. As you open your eyes, all you see is clutter. Your bedside table has a mug of coffee on it from days gone by. You knock over a pile of unread books while you're trying to find the off button on your alarm, and then scatter a pile of papers from last night's WFH session onto the floor...

Somehow you avoid stepping on your laptop as you stumble to the bathroom. You skip over the damp towel from yesterday's shower, which is in a heap on the floor because there was nowhere to hang it. It's starting to smell musty but no doubt will stay there until the weekend when you have time to tackle the laundry... if you have time. Of course, you only realize the loo roll has run out and no one has replaced it once it's too late. On the side, the Jenga tower of cleanser tubs, all half-used, threatens to topple into the toilet. In contrast to the glut of beauty products, you can't find your toothpaste and when you do unearth it, the lid is cemented to the tube with crusty residue. Where are your pills?

Where are your pills? Who knows? You give up.

Back in the bedroom, finding a pair of knickers without holes is as likely as a lottery win, while none of your bras work with your planned outfit. Your shirt needs an iron and there's a button missing. Shoes that match your handbag are a distant dream.

Why is everything such an effort? Downstairs, you lurch into the kitchen, stepping on a rogue Lego block in the hall. Locating the cornflakes is surprisingly easy but as you yank the box out of the cupboard you dislodge the other packets stacked on top of it and are showered with cereal. The milk is off, obviously, and as chaos swells around you, you remember that you have that really important presentation at work today. Once you've finally bundled yourself into the car, you reach for one of the dozen water bottles rolling wildly around the back seat. Which is the freshest is anyone's guess. They all taste stale. By the time you arrive at the office you are in a world of stress but don't know why.

Sound familiar? You have just experienced the Trail of Destruction. Every day is the same. There are never any fresh towels because you never get to the bottom of the laundry basket. You haven't had a moment to slow down, let alone get your best work shoes reheeled. And while you might not think taking those coffee mugs out of your bedroom affects how professional you appear at work, how well you get on with your partner or how well you sleep at night, let me enlighten you.

Hello, I'm Dilly Carter...

... a professional organizer and the founder of Declutter Dollies – a comprehensive organizing and home-styling service that promises to turn people's chaos into calm. My job is to go into people's houses, offices and workspaces and help them create structure so they become more organized. I've zhuzhed the homes of A-List actors, authors and fitness influencers with millions of followers. I've helped celebrity make-up artists move house and unpacked everything so as they walk in there are candles burning and flowers in vases. I work with everyone, from CEOs of companies worth millions of pounds, to busy mums. I can tackle a mansion but I also overhaul small kitchens or wardrobes in two hours.

When I organize, I don't just arrange things aesthetically and make sure everyone knows where everything is, I reset the approach on how you live. There are other books on creating an organized home but this one is different.

I can show you how to organize your jars neatly, but after you read this book you're going to know how your home really operates. I want to provide the tools to empower you and give you back control of your whole life, not just in your home, but in your mind.

When your house is clear, you can see things afresh, as well as having a fresh new look in your home. When someone gets back on top of their home, it's a life-changing moment. If you've fallen out of love with your house, you can fall back in love. Where clutter reigns, you can regain control of your space.

Proper organization can make you feel like you've moved into a brand new house. I will show you how you can live with less and take control of your spending. The key is that you really don't need as much stuff as you think you do. Our cupboards don't need to be stuffed with food. Not every wardrobe has to be crammed to overflowing. I've seen how people can live with very little. Being able to breathe in your home and have a calm environment to relax in is really important.

When you have more physical space around you, you have more space in your head.

Compared to the serene sanctuaries I help my clients transform their homes into, I grew up in very different circumstances. I was born into chaos and my life experiences have taught me that there is an obvious link between clutter and mental clarity. Until I was three I lived in an orphanage in Sri Lanka, surrounded by the noise of children shouting, playing and running everywhere. My existence was empty of toys but I was loved. I came to England in 1983 and was raised by my wonderful adoptive mum and dad. But the chaos continued as their house was always untidy. All the time.

My dad was an accountant and my mum worked alongside him in all manner of roles. Although they had an office in Southall, they also did a lot of work from home and the house was always full of paperwork. My dad mainly worked from the dining room table and you could never see the surface of it. Their bedroom was the same. You couldn't even see the floor! I found the mess stressful and, especially in my early teens, I often felt embarrassed about the state of the house. But there was one big advantage: my house became the party house! My parents were so laid-back because they were always working – they never minded who came round or at what time!

I constantly tried to tidy my parents' mess but I was always told off for moving the papers around. They were the adults so there wasn't much I could do about the situation. They weren't open to change and I was just a child. Instead, I spent as little time as possible at home or retreated to my bedroom (which was immaculate). I found my happy place at our neighbour's house as it was the complete opposite of my own home. They were a tight family unit and their house, always immaculate and organized, was what I dreamed my home would be like. Looking back, it's now very clear that I craved organization and so as soon as I could leave home, I did. I didn't have to live amongst my parents' chaos anymore, and while I loved them, I was so happy to just be in control of me.

Think about your home. Are you trying to escape?

Does your home make you feel heavy, tired or depressed? How can you change that?

When you look round your house and think, 'I'm miserable', how does that affect your relationships? What is the biggest stress point? Is it clothes on the bedroom floor, books overflowing from the shelves, messy cupboards in the kitchen? Perhaps your partner has taken over the spare room and nothing gets put away so you're constantly arguing? Or are you the messy one and can't get your head around where to put things?

This book will give you a reality check and get your whole life in order, but you need to be honest. Identify who the issue is with. Where is the problem? Why is it an issue? Work through those feelings. They may go all the way back to childhood like mine do. But if you're ready to look under the surface of the clutter, it will change your life.

Reclaim
Your
Space

Less is more

Minimizing what you have will give you control. Less stuff means less to do. Less cleaning, less tidying. So living a more minimal life will give you back time. One of the reasons you're constantly tidying your kids' toys is because they have too many. If your child only had three or four toys, you'd only be picking up three or four, but the reality is that we have to pick up 50 or 60. As adults, we are the ones consuming, we are the ones in charge of how many toys we buy our children.

The only reason our houses are messy is because of our own overconsumption of toys, clothes, food, cleaning products... Society needs to slow down. We need to stop buying. We need to be mindful and only buy what we really need. For instance, rather than just automatically repeat-buying your groceries each week, plan your meals ahead and look at what you have in your fridge before you shop.

Buying blind

When people buy things that they don't need, because they don't know what they already have, I call this 'buying blind'. It's so important to think (and look!) at what you already have before buying more. This is an essential point for every room in your house. (And for the planet; think about *where* you're buying from too.)

Space and wellbeing

Throughout my childhood I watched as my mum struggled with her mental health – not only working with my dad and the stress that caused, but also from not being able to get on top of things at home. It wasn't until my dad died in 2013 and I visited Mum in her new home that I saw how ill she was. If my childhood home was messy, Mum's new house was on a different level. During her worst bipolar episodes she had been a victim of fraud and given away £50,000 to scammers. I started to clear out her house and there were boxes of pills, stacks of face creams, a carrier bag full of iTunes cards with the barcodes scratched off... She'd been sending four-figure MoneyGrams to Hong Kong and Spain. Without my dad to look after her, she could only just get into bed (which was covered in cat hair), and you couldn't see the sofa or surfaces. Her space reflected her mental state.

It was the most horrendous way to live so I moved her to the home I shared with my husband and baby daughter. As I cleared her house I had the realization that there are so many people who have to move piles of paperwork just to watch TV or, even worse, can't watch TV until they've pulled out a foldaway chair because there is so much stuff on their sofa they can't actually sit down on it. Cluttered, uncomfortable spaces hold us back, make us more anxious and have a negative impact on our wellbeing.

Mental clutter

Perhaps it's time for you to realize that being untidy is more than a personality trait. The issues that follow me from my childhood stem from something deeper than just growing up with untidy parents. Perhaps you're here for advice on arranging one room? I can help you start with that, but you may need to deal with something more extreme.

You could live in a million-pound house or rent a bedsit, but the way you're feeling will have a real effect on your home. If you are not in the right place mentally, then your home is never going to be in the right place. If you can identify that you're unhappy, it's a great start, but there are still things to address. Before we begin your organizing journey, ask yourself if you are ready to do the work. Why aren't you happy in your home right now? Can you change that? How can you change it? Do you need help to change it?

How this book works

When you feel ready to work through this book, I want you to realize how vital the space you inhabit is to your entire life – your work, your relationships, and your mental health.

I want you to understand how every room connects to the rest of the house. If someone sends me a picture of their wardrobe and asks for help, I need to see the bigger picture. What else is in the space? Is there a chest of drawers? What about underbed storage? Can they access a loft?

To correct one room, we need to look at the whole space and make it flow. That's why reading – and ideally working through – this book chapter by chapter is the best way to benefit from my experience and advice. The way the chapters are arranged is the way we experience our rooms day to day. So read it in order and do the work.

In every room I want you to honestly answer the following set of fundamental questions. Mark this page and refer back to it before you tackle any space.

4 Fundamental Questions for Every Room

- » **What is your vision for this room?**
- » **Does this room reflect who you are?**
- » **Can you tackle this alone?**
- » **Are you ready to set aside a full day to tackle it?**

Time for a Dolly Dash

Inside these pages you won't find quick fixes and hacks because my approach to organization is deeper than that. But you will find lots of storage solutions, sorting tips, '101' advice pages, and speedy decluttering tasks that I like to call 'Dolly Dashes'.

A Dolly Dash is a 15-minute challenge to change something in your home. Regularly organizing small areas will help you keep on top of the clutter and keep things organized. You might think that 15 minutes isn't enough time to make any real difference, but it really will encourage you to make a start on decluttering.

You might give the sock drawer dash a whirl (see page 42). Once you have finished the sense of achievement might drive you on to declutter the chest of drawers, perhaps you'll even be inspired to tackle the whole room. You'll find Dolly Dash ideas at the end of each chapter. Look out for the clock symbol and take your pick of any of the 15-minute dashes listed on that page.

Chip Away at Disarray

Each Dolly Dash has four simple stages...

» **Empty the space and clean it.**
» **Go through the items and organize them into groups according to type.**
» **Sort through the 'Three Rs': rubbish to throw away; items to recycle; and items to return to their rightful place.**
» **Return the items to the space in their groups.**

Don't just make it pretty, make it work

When you think about your answers to those questions in each room, compare the reality of the space to how you imagined it would be when you moved in. Use that mental picture as your end goal and always keep it in mind as you work your way through every room. It will help you stay on track – even when you reach that inevitable moment when you wish you hadn't started!

As you work your way through the pages – and subsequently the rooms in your house – you'll think profoundly and realize things about your life that you didn't even consider before:

Is this why my relationship is like this?
Is this why I feel tired all the time?
Is this why my space is in a mess?

As you work through each room you'll see how little actions can bring about huge positive changes in the rest of your life. Decluttering will enable you to make the most of your home and give you the headspace to breathe, to think, to live. Ultimately, I hope this book will help you clear, change and create space.

Ready?
Let's do this...

A TALE OF CHAOS TO CALM

Calm and curated

'I had been decluttering a day at a time since January under my own steam but had lost heart. The loft area in particular was a job too far. I followed Declutter Dollies on Instagram and knew how lovely Dilly was. I had also seen the before and after pictures and knew she would be perfect to reinvigorate my space. Before she arrived, Dilly FaceTimed me to look over the house. This was brilliant as she suggested things I needed to do, which inspired me for the next day. She arrived at 9am and we worked together until 1pm. In those four hours we completely transformed the loft.

Dilly has an amazing ability to assess a room with one glance. I had been an antiques dealer and had many objects scattered around the room in a very incoherent manner and things had built up over time. Dilly grouped my belongings, creating a logical flow to the room, which is very calming and pleasing to the eye. I had been worried that I would be left with nothing but that was not the case. Dilly said she was happy to leave my bookcases as they were because they reflected my personality and style. I like to think of Dilly as a curator. Once she finished decluttering she displayed my possessions in the most beautiful fashion. I have tried to continue to refresh the house using Dilly's principles and I have succeeded for the most part.

It is now beautiful again, clutter-free, calm and relaxing. Dilly doesn't just help you decide what to let go of, she actually has an amazing eye for pinpointing exactly how you can organize all the different areas of your home. I cannot recommend Dilly highly enough. I am booking another session to work on other areas of our house. I feel lighter, happier and grin every morning when I go upstairs to the loft to look at the beautiful space we have up there now. Dilly is an absolute wonder! She really is a saviour!'

Reclaim Your Headspace 101

Every chapter in this book will show you how you can utilize the space in your house in a better way. But really, the key to being organized is to not have as much stuff in the first place. When you're constantly having to find space for growing collections but aren't willing to acknowledge that you simply have too much stuff, there is a deeper problem.

That is why decluttering is so important as well as being organized. You really need to look at what is in your home and admit that you've accumulated too much over the years. To change the space, you need to reduce the stuff. But your mental health is often the cause of the clutter. There are so many emotions attached to material possessions. Perhaps you're hanging onto items you don't want or need because they hold memories of a loved one and you don't feel ready to let them go?

There are also countless reasons why people buy too much and, again, it's all attached to our mental health. Depression is probably one of the biggest reasons people overbuy things. People buy a little treat for themselves when they feel down. You feel sad so need to do something to make yourself feel better. I've been to homes where there are 40 to 50 big plastic tubs full of beauty products that can never be used in one person's lifetime – but each purchase was made to improve someone's mood.

I've also organized in houses where there were so many clothes it was overwhelming, even for me. There are many of us who are undiagnosed shopaholics. We often joke about being one but if you are, it is not a joke. It can soon become a big problem in many relationships and men and women are equally likely to suffer from the compulsion to shop.

I have a friend whose boyfriend is a shopaholic and he has so many clothes. He has 40 shirts on each hanger and his spare bedroom is full of at least 50 boxes of new deliveries still to be opened. Every day more packages arrive. His stuff is even taking over his mum's house as it no longer fits in their home. But he still can't see he has a problem. My friend has pointed out that he has 300 pairs of trainers, including multiple colours of the same brand. Wow. You might think that's insane, but here is the real problem: the bedrooms are now so overrun with clothes that his son can't stay over in his own room due to lack of space. Shopping is an addiction and a major issue that affects the whole family.

People often become addicted to shopping because of the impact it has on their mental state. Buying makes us feel good: the adrenalin rush, the promise of newness. We rarely shop out of necessity but we all need to bring back the balance between needing and wanting to shop. We need to learn to soothe ourselves not by hitting the 'Buy it Now' button, but by appreciating and taking care of the things we already have.

So as well as physically organizing and decluttering, you have to be in control of yourself and stop overspending. Look at the space you live in before you go shopping. So many people buy like they are living in a four-bedroom house instead of the one-bed flat they actually live in. Should you really buy another pair of shoes if you have nowhere to put them? If you want a new dress, do you need to donate or sell one you already own first? Whether we're buying clothes, shoes, handbags, make-up, canned goods, kitchen equipment or cleaning products, we always need to apply the same golden rule:

Use what you have before you buy more.

Always be really truthful with yourself about your reasons for buying before you spend. You may need to sacrifice the short-term buzz you get from buying new things, but the long-term satisfaction and sense of wellbeing you will gain once you're saving money and living in an organized, clutter-free space will more than make up for it. Your house won't just be tidier, it will be cleaner too – because it's always easier to make clear surfaces shine or glasses in a tidy cupboard sparkle. The whole space will be better for you. You'll feel lighter, brighter and more in control. Instead of feeling anxious about the mounting chores (and bills), you'll feel relaxed and on top of things. You'll have more time – to take care of yourself and to be with your friends and family. When you declutter your home, you clear your mind to reclaim healthier, happier headspace.

It's so important to look after your mental health. Please see pages 180–181 for more information on organizations that can offer support.

Bedroom

This book begins with the bedroom as it's the first room you encounter on the Trail of Destruction, but we also start here because sleep is essential to our health. Any good therapist or doctor will tell you that sleep is vital for wellbeing, so if you're not getting a good night's sleep could the chaos in your bedroom be contributing to that? Your bedroom is the first place you see when you wake and the last thing you see at night. It should be inviting, calm, a sanctuary. Going to bed surrounded by stuff, or in an uninviting room, is stressful and can affect the quality of your sleep far more than you might realize.

When I was growing up, I saw my mum and dad struggle with their work lives and poor health. The two factors were directly associated and, to make things worse, they lived and tried to sleep amongst the mess. Their bedroom was definitely not a place to relax. My bedroom was the complete opposite. It was always immaculate. I was constantly changing things round, moving the furniture, trying to create space. I even painted the walls a deep red while they were out.

My parents worked so hard and I saw first-hand how the state of the house had a negative effect on them. Walking into their room was beyond stressful! The décor was dated, the bed was the opposite of inviting and the whole space felt chaotic. How my dad could have such a professional job but could barely find clean pants in the morning was a mystery. I would always try and tidy up for them but it quickly became a mess again. It was an ongoing argument. Seeing the way they lived just confirmed that I wanted the exact opposite for myself.

During my childhood my mum also spent a lot of time in hospital and it's one of the places that reminds me just how stark a bedroom can be. There was a bed, a chest of drawers and a Bible. That was it. Likewise, when I look back at the photos from my time in the orphanage, I just had a basic metal cot. There was a blanket but nothing else. We come into this world with very little and really, we don't need much. While these are extreme examples of

stripping back a space, they are also a wake-up call that you need to get back to basics. Look at your room as if it was brand new to you. What do you really need?

And is your bedroom a reflection of who you are? I work with people from all social backgrounds across the UK and organize everything from studio flats to houses worth £30 million. One thing I've noticed is how many people in corporate positions don't have homes that reflect their public image. In their wardrobe there will be a solitary shirt hanging from a dodgy hanger, none of their socks will match and good luck finding a pair without holes in them. If people could see how they live they wouldn't believe they made it past the job interview!

> ## Once your bedroom is organized, it should be the most relaxing and tranquil space in the house.

Bedrooms are far more important than we give them credit for. If you could have a better home life, imagine how much better your work life could be! Once your bedroom (and wardrobe) is sorted you'll feel clearer, more focused and everything will run smoothly from the minute you wake up to the minute you get to work.

Make Your Bedroom Your Sanctuary

When you walk into your bedroom you should think: I just want to curl up in that bed and go to sleep. A comfortable pillow, the right duvet, clean sheets that feel inviting... What you don't want to think is: what a pit, where do I start? If that's the case, you just end up crawling into bed (and crawling back out) every single day. The fact that you're reading this book means you're ready for a kick-start. Before we begin to transform your room, ask yourself the questions at the bottom of page 27.

If you don't like your answers to any of those questions, I want to help you. The questions aren't meant to guilt you into tidying up, but give you a reality check of how you could feel if you make a change. Proper organization should make you feel on top of everything, give you back time and help you save money. Ultimately you will feel better and have more control.

What I want you to achieve is the feeling that your bedroom is like a hotel room.

Think about when you're staying away somewhere. We feel that sensation of relaxation so readily because hotel rooms are basically empty. There's a bed, a chest of drawers, a side table and lamp – the minimum that you need. And you'll have the best night's sleep. Yes, I know it's a completely different situation to home because your kids might not be there... or your snoring partner... but the basis of a hotel room is minimalism. That's why when we flick through home magazines and holiday brochures everything looks so calm. There's nothing there! Similarly, when you look at adverts for wardrobes you don't see the clutter of reality, you just see a serene bedroom.

That's what we need to recreate in our homes and this is why it's important to create a sanctuary that replicates that hotel room feeling. Everything needs to belong in its own organized space. The room should smell fresh and the sheets should be clean, with the bed dressed beautifully and the pillows fluffed.

Think about how you can create that environment in your room. For instance, it's really important to air your bedroom and think about the lighting. Do you need dim mood lighting? Perhaps change up the overhead bulb for lamps and a dimmer switch to make it a place where you can truly relax and read a book. Perhaps you need fresh bedding or new pillows too. (Get rid of those yellow flat pillows you haven't changed for ages!) When did you last treat yourself to new sheets? So many people overlook the importance of correctly fitting, comfortable sheets. You could also have a beautiful candle and one special picture. Maybe these little things feel like they are at the bottom of your to-do list but, as I said at the start of this chapter, a good night's sleep is so important.

Does This Space Make Me Feel Happy?

» Is my bedroom what I imagined it would be when I moved in?
» Are there mugs on the surfaces and clothes all over the floor?
» Does it look like an adult's bedroom or could it be mistaken for a teenager's room?
» Is the washing basket overflowing?
» Is there a chair for clothes I've worn but that aren't clean enough to go back in the wardrobe?
» Are there 25 unread books stacked next to the bed?
» If you're in a relationship: how is my wardrobe arranged versus my partner's?
» If you're single: am I happy for someone to open my wardrobe doors?
» What would a guest think if they looked in my wardrobe? Would I feel embarrassed?

Surprising Things That Might Affect Your Sleep

Paperwork

Your bedroom might be the only place you can work but having a stack of unopened mail or paperwork by your bed will cause you stress – and have a negative impact on your sleep. Anything that remains yet to be actioned will hang over you. There shouldn't be anything on your bedside table except a couple of books, a lamp and whatever else you need hidden in a drawer.

Do you and your partner have little or no intimacy? Is it because your bedroom is uninviting? Clutter has a huge impact on relationships. We all know that we argue with our partners when they leave their pants on the floor and they don't get picked up for days. But what you think are just 'little' things are actually major issues which affect your whole relationship and can spread to your work life too. Think about it. Perhaps your relationship is stressful because your house is out of control or chaotic?

Overflowing laundry

Anything you can see that needs to be done will make your subconscious mind anxious. You know you need to tackle the washing but you're too busy. If you're waiting for the weekend, remove the laundry from your eyeline. Once it's out of sight, it's out of mind.

When you get round to it, laundry should only ever take a day to catch up on. If it takes two to three days, you need to look at how much you have. People who never see the bottom of their laundry baskets aren't just time-poor. If you can never catch up with the washing it's because you have too many clothes, you're wearing them too much and washing them too often. If you have four kids, yes there will be a lot more laundry – but how many outfits are they wearing a day?

Organizing your home is not just about keeping your laundry basket under control and storing things neatly, it's thinking deeply about how you function in your house. It's recognizing how our lifestyle affects the way we behave and how we teach our children to behave.

Too much make-up

I see so many spaces full of disorganized beauty products that are taking up way too much space. If you're guilty of over-consumption of things – be it beauty products or clothes – it will affect the way your bedroom flows and how you sleep.

Make sure your bedroom surfaces are clear. Only have beautiful things on display. Reinvent the space you have and if you can make your products look aesthetically pleasing, that will add to the value of your sleep. Can you create a lovely arrangement of, say, perfume bottles or scented candles on a mirrored glass tray? Imagine waking up and only seeing beautiful things on the side rather than a dispiriting jumble of 60 different face creams.

If you are someone that has lots of beauty products, you need to find somewhere to house them so they are organized and out of sight. Although if you love £200 face creams from Barbara Sturm, perhaps you want to put up a glass shelf to display them? I think make-up should always be in an organizer (you can easily find acrylic ones online) or you could buy a chest of drawers that you can divide up.

If you love make-up, you'll need something that really showcases your addiction. Make-up artist Lisa Potter-Dixon went to Kempton Park antiques fair and found the most beautiful, huge,

vintage organizer for her products, which I helped her arrange. Whether you spend £500 on Ikea drawers that you can split up or you only have five different products in one make-up bag (like me), however you store your products will generally reflect the quality of your relationship with those products.

Random items

Have you got an exercise bike in your bedroom? Is the cardboard box your kitchen mixer came in lurking at the bottom of your wardrobe? Are there suitcases propped up beside your chest of drawers? Any random items in your bedroom will ultimately affect the storage space you have for clothes. This can then have a knock-on effect on the rest of your room, which could also impact the quality of your sleep.

Identify the clutter you're storing in your bedroom and take it out. Find a proper home for it, whether that's the garage, spare room or loft – or a charity shop or recycling centre. Everything in your bedroom should belong there. Maybe your chest of drawers is filled with a jumble of papers and products. If you emptied the drawers, you'd be able to fit your clothes in. Audit your wardrobe. Do those memory boxes need to live there? Take them out and create a proper home for all your shoes. Everything remaining should have its place.

Shop Smarter and Question Your Fashion Buys

Quality not quantity

The ultimate goal is to have fewer things. When you're clothes shopping, prioritize quality not quantity. Buy cheap? Buy twice. This philosophy should run through your entire house from big-ticket items like furniture to little accessories like picture frames – it's not just for purchasing clothes. Always think about why you want to buy something and work out what is more valuable. Is it a single 'wow' moment when everyone compliments you, or being able to wear something again and again that you love?

Over six years ago I bought a leopard-print Givenchy tote bag. I love it and use it all the time. When it broke, I sent it back to Givenchy and they fixed it so it's brand new again. The bag has lasted the test of time and is the perfect example that, when possible, we should always buy quality things that are designed to last.

The Saturday Test

Avoiding impulse buys is also important. Whenever you're tempted to shop, do what I call 'The Saturday Test'. Say it's a Monday and you're in work and scrolling the New In section of your favourite brand. You see a dress and you want it! You need it! Immediately! Hang on, hold off pressing Buy Now. What makes you want to buy it instantly? Often, if you have to wait, you'll change your mind or move on to something else. Test yourself. Don't buy it but see how you feel on Saturday when your mood is very different to Monday. If you're still thinking about it and would make the journey to a shop to try it on, it will be the right choice. Only buying things that pass The Saturday Test will give you a wardrobe of pieces you really love because you have proved that you truly want them. You need to have a burning desire and think you cannot live without something for it to be worthy of a place in your wardrobe.

Invest in a capsule wardrobe

Our clothes are so important to our state of mind. Everything from our underwear outwards can change our mood and every item can work as a layer of confidence. See your clothes as an investment and make sure you buy to suit your shape. Visit a personal shopper or stylist if that will help you. Investing in quality pieces you love is particularly important with clothes because if you decide to sell something in the future, you want items that will hold their value. Cultivating a capsule wardrobe will help you do this.

We have seen a huge shift towards a slower fashion system, and fast fashion is no longer just uncool, it's bad for the environment and your bank balance. Society is waking up to the fact that we don't need a new outfit every weekend and the rental fashion sector is fast becoming the coolest solution – you can go to that event in your dream dress, but avoid the nightmare price tag.

Once you've done a major clean out, don't go out and buy a whole new wardrobe! I know sometimes you'll be tempted but whenever you're considering a new buy, use The Saturday Test and work out how many things the new purchase would go with. Can you mix and match that top with all your jeans and smart trousers? Could it go with three things immediately? Or is it so much of a statement it will only suit one skirt? Everything must earn its place.

The best version of yourself

This section isn't just about teaching you how to declutter your wardrobe, I want you to realize why the things you had before didn't work so you never make those mistakes again. Perhaps you feel you're not getting noticed at work. Is it because you're not wearing suits that fit? Maybe you don't feel like the best version of yourself.

If you don't dress the way you feel, you won't be empowered. Every item of clothing you own should make you feel incredible. Go through your clothes (see page 32). Sell what you don't like or give it to charity. Once you've done a clear-out, you should have a wardrobe full of things you absolutely love, and because you'll have space you could invest in a few really good quality additions as and when you need to. Slowly, you'll build a capsule wardrobe that makes you feel like 'you'.

Love everything you own

This is the time to be really honest with yourself. Does your wardrobe make you happy when you open it? Can you list everything in your wardrobe? Do you really know what you have? When was the last time you bought something? When was your last really good clear-out? The goal is to reduce the things in your wardrobe and leave it filled only with items you love.

Building a feel-good wardrobe is about picking a capsule collection of pieces you can mix and match. One pair of Christian Louboutin Pigalle courts that go with all your skirts and jeans are worth more (in every sense) than six pairs of heels from the high street. Remember, ultimately we want to reduce what's in your wardrobe and choose quality over quantity whenever we can.

Work your way through each item in your wardrobe, asking yourself the questions below. Only keep the best! Return the clothes you want to keep to the wardrobe – these are the items you really love. Then make one pile of clothes to donate and one pile to resell. (For advice on donating items responsibly, see page 182. For advice on reselling, see page 183.)

Always ask yourself why you want to keep a particular item or give it away. Generally, the things we love are those we spent the most on. We're quick to throw away cheap high street buys while the most treasured pieces are likely to be the most expensive. That's why it's so important to buy quality clothes that will last rather than fast fashion fixes you'll only wear once before throwing them to the bottom of your wardrobe.

How Do I Look?

Go through every single item in your wardrobe and ask yourself the following:

- » When did I last wear it?
- » Will I wear it again?
- » How does it make me feel?
- » Does it fit?
- » Do I like the style?
- » Does it suit me?
- » Do I have multiples of the same thing?
- » Should I keep, sell, donate or recycle this item?

I find people often live in a house they have in their head. They think they're living in a mansion and need 500 pairs of shoes because of their job as a blogger. But the reality is, they live in a one-bed flat in Tottenham, and they don't have space for all those shoes. You have to be sensible about what you have – and what you have room for. Even if you think you've been working hard and deserve those shoes and you can afford them, have you got the space?

Of course now and then I buy stuff from the high street, but only if it's something like a plain black linen dress that is going to last me a few seasons. I don't buy many clothes and if I'm going out, I often rent things. If I do buy fashion it's usually shoes or bags and I'll spend money on something timeless that I will keep and use year after year.

How to Arrange a Feel-good Wardrobe

1 Change with the seasons
Once you've decided what you're keeping (see page 32) you're ready to go. If you can, start by dividing your clothes by seasons and rotate your wardrobe. If you're trying to house a whole year's worth of clothes in one wardrobe you'll trip up. There's no point having clothes in your wardrobe that you're not going to wear for six months.

Winter coats take up so much room and if it's not the right season you'll lose lots of storage space. If you can, put up a rail in your loft or spare room for out of season clothes. If they are hanging you will be able to access them easily instead of scrambling through boxes or suitcases. Get a rail protector and they'll stay clean until it's time to bring them down.

If you only have one wardrobe and can't move items elsewhere, make sure you arrange everything by weight – from heavy to light.

2 Choose storage solutions that suit you
Be realistic. Maybe you travel all year round for your job so you need to see your summer things in November. Whatever storage solutions you choose, they need to suit your lifestyle.

I meet a lot of people who have stored their clothes in tubs or vacuum packs. They do save space but you can never properly see what's inside until you open them. When we store things in the loft or spare room, fast-forward five years and often we have forgotten what's there. That's why it's really important to think about access when you are considering the right storage solutions for you.

3 Kit out your wardrobe
Before you start to arrange your feel-good wardrobe, look at the space. Are you using it effectively? Do you need to move shelves or adjust their height? Do you need more rails? What do you want this space to do? How do you imagine it? Do whatever you need to do to achieve the image in your head – and don't stop until it's done. Buy any supplies you need like hangers, clip hangers, baskets, drawer dividers or hanging rails. When possible, always use slimline velvet hangers, not wooden, to maximize the space. (See page 168 for more advice.)

4 Reset your wardrobe

Block out a morning to tackle the job. When you're ready to go, whack on some tunes and empty the wardrobe, so you're starting from a blank space. Clean the rails, vacuum the floor and adjust the rails or shelves if you need to.

5 Structure is the new black

Now you can start to hang your clothes and it's all about structure. Begin with heavy coats (if it's the right season), then pea coats, followed by leather jackets, denim jackets, bomber jackets and blazers. Then move onto long-sleeve shirts, then long-sleeve dresses. Next, hang your short-sleeve shirts. Your wardrobe should get physically shorter and lighter until you end with strappy vests. Left to right arrangements look aesthetically pleasing and when you group items in sections it's easier to see everything you have. One exception to this rule: put skirts and trousers to the left of coats. If they are in the middle of the rail it'll break up the aesthetic. Make sure you keep them on clip hangers.

Once you've grouped everything within each section, then organize by type. Hang silk blouses together and denim shirts together. If you're really into brands you might group Rixo dresses or All Saints jackets together. However you organize your clothes, again, it must work for you. I want to give you the tools for organization but how you actually arrange things has to make sense for your life. If you always wear certain tops and skirts together, it might work to group them by outfit.

Unless you have a huge walk-in wardrobe, never organize in colour. You can arrange colours within a group of the same items, but hanging a block of yellow means you'll end up searching for one piece within those bigger groups, which slows down the whole process. The whole point of organization is to give you back time.

6 Fold 'n' roll

You can also store things in drawers or on shelves – either rolled or file folded – and add drawer dividers to separate soft jersey items like socks, pyjamas and sports bras. Successful storage always depends on the individual area so ask yourself: what is the best way to use this space? I've found that many people don't know how to properly fold their clothes. Pages 36–39 show you how to do this.

File folding stores your clothes upright, meaning any logos are visible. I'd only ever roll leggings, tracksuit bottoms or jeans but however you fold things, make sure items are still grouped. You could arrange your jeans the way your favourite store presents them (graduated from light washes to dark indigo) or you could arrange them by brand. If you have space you could also hang jeans on clip hangers if that works within your wardrobe layout.

Rolling jeans

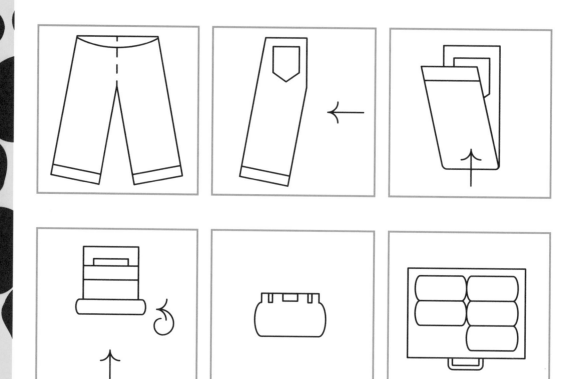

File folding T-shirts

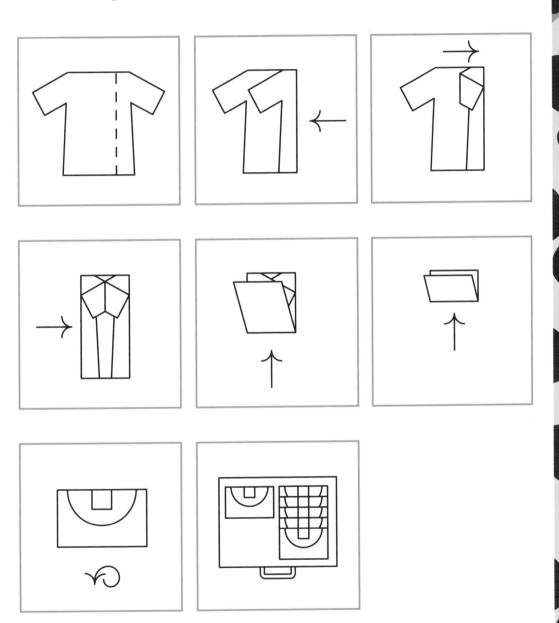

File folding shirts

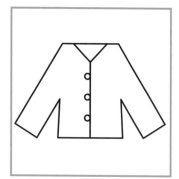

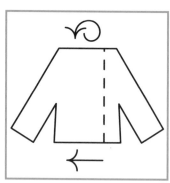

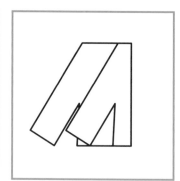

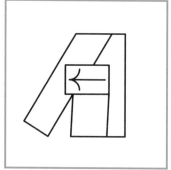

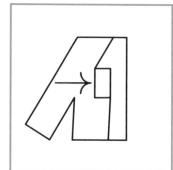

7 Storing shoes and bags

If you're a shoe (or bag) lover you'll want to have everything beautifully displayed. If you have lots of bags and shoes, the ultimate storage solution is a display wall. Floating shelving will give you that walk-in wardrobe feel but if you don't have space, put your shoes in boxes and your handbags inside dust covers (which will protect expensive items). It's also good if you can stuff your handbags with supports or tissue paper to help them keep their shape. The main thing is to store your shoes and bags so you can clearly see what you have. Again, the right storage solution will depend on the volume you have.

If you don't want to display your shoes, keep them in neatly stacked boxes at the bottom of the wardrobe. You can put Polaroids on the outside of the boxes or buy clear boxes from Ikea so you know what's inside. And don't forget the space outside your bedroom too. Perhaps you have an unused under-stairs cupboard you could put shelves in for shoe or accessory storage?

8 All about accessories

You will need to group other accessories together as efficiently as possible. Bobble hats and baseball caps can go in a basket on top of the wardrobe, while big hats could be hung on a hook on the door. I love using rails for scarves. At one house I tied all the silk scarves onto brass rails, but it always depends on what sort of scarf it is. Silk scarves also look beautiful organized and rolled in a basket but stay clear of scarf hangers (the type that hold the scarf by poking it through a hole) as they will end up looking messy. I keep my one woolly scarf in a box in my porch as I only wear it outside and can grab it on my way out.

Only by gutting and stripping back your wardrobe will you be able to truly value what you have and ensure your wardrobe only contains things that you love. Your bedroom should now be a calm space where you can rest and wake up feeling relaxed and ready for the day ahead. When you open your wardrobe, you should feel happy – and able to find a top that matches that skirt with ease.

Packing 101

Now you've decluttered your bedroom and wardrobe, everything you're going to take on holiday will come from your perfectly edited closet of clothes that always makes you feel great. Your summer wardrobe will be made up of items you love, so putting together your holiday case should never be a struggle.

We live a very minimal life on holiday. We usually wear the same flip flops, the same shorts, the same dress... so holiday packing is a great lesson in putting together a capsule wardrobe. If we take just a few things, we can mix and match that one silk slip dress with different shoes or jewellery.

If you have some time before your trip, try to plan your outfits for the seven days (or however long you're going to be away). Use a hanging rail to help you if you have one. Once you've finished, you're going to feel more in control and organized.

The best way to pack a suitcase is to roll and fold and use packing cubes wherever you can. I always use the roll and fold methods (see pages 36–39), the clothes are stored neatly and stay almost crease-free so they just need to be hung when you arrive.

Packing cubes let you organize your suitcase beautifully so you can arrange everything in sections and don't open your case to chaos. You can put all your swimsuits together, your underwear, your tops, bottoms, dresses – or if you have already planned your outfits, you can pack them together in the cubes. You need to create structure in your suitcase, just like we did in your wardrobe.

There is often a lining at the bottom of your suitcase. Many people don't use it but it forms a very useful layer between your clothes and your shoes. Unzip it and tuck your shoes in between the outer case and the lining. Because there is generally a groove to the suitcase, your shoes will fit perfectly! If you can keep your suitcase organized, when you arrive on holiday everything will be easy to find and you can relax and really enjoy yourself.

Clutter

We always want to have our bedroom feeling calm so it's especially important you keep on top of the clutter that can build up. Start by gathering up all the washing and take it to the laundry basket. Put away any clothes hanging off the side of your bed. Clear the surfaces of any cups and mugs and tidy away excess make-up you might have left out. Make your bed. I can't believe I have to say this but so many people don't make their beds every day! Puff up the pillows and neaten the pile of books on your side table.

Sock Drawer

Start by emptying your sock drawer completely. Wipe out any dust or fluff lurking in the corners and go through every single sock, making sure they are all matched up in pairs. If you have odd socks, don't throw them away – you can use them as rags and dusters. Likewise, all the socks that have worn through and have holes can be used as cleaning cloths too. Once all your socks are matched up, group them into sections by type: so you have your sports socks together, colourful socks together, black socks together, striped socks together... Add a divider into the drawer so you can separate each section and keep them tidy moving forward.

Dolly Dash

Sleepwear

Empty out your sleepwear drawer then group everything so you have a section for your pyjama sets, your bottoms, loungewear and nighties. Put anything that is a matching set together and fold all your pyjamas neatly. I like to fold beautiful sets together, generally in a drawer, but if you have just bottoms then roll them (see pages 36–39). It all depends on the volume of items you own.

Underwear

Start by taking everything out of the drawer and wiping round to get rid of any lurking dust. Get rid of anything tatty and old – you want to dispose of anything you can get rid of to make the space bright and clear for the items you want to keep. If you have any old bras that no longer fit you – but are still in good condition – donate them to a bra bank (see page 182). Once you've been through all your underwear, group the bras into sections like seamfree, lace, shaping, push-up, and cotton. Line up the bras in each group in colour order from dark to light. Return the bras to the drawer keeping everything upright so you can see exactly what you have. Separate your pants into lace, silk, cotton and break these down by colour and style. I finish by folding vests and camisoles and laying them at the back of the drawer.

Regroup Your Wardrobe

Regrouping your wardrobe is a really effective and satisfying Dolly Dash at the start or end of the working week. Make sure all your jackets, shirts, dresses and so on are hanging together and easy to find. I also love using this time to switch the way things are stored around. You could move your jeans from hanging to having them rolled in drawers (see page 36).

Bedroom Checklist

CREATE A TRANQUIL SANCTUARY AND GET A GOOD NIGHT'S SLEEP

☐ **A place for everything and everything in its place**
Every item in your bedroom needs to belong in its own organized space. Keep the items on your bedside table to the bare minimum – a couple of books, a lamp – and leave anything else you need hidden away in a drawer.

☐ **Hotel at home**
Make your bedroom feel like a boutique hotel room. Add some mood lighting, flowers or a candle with a soothing fragrance to recreate that relaxing environment and get a luxurious night's sleep.

☐ **Dress the bed beautifully**
Fluff the pillows, change the bedding, treat yourself to quality sheets, review your bedding regularly (out with those flat yellow pillows!) and replace when you need to. Everything should smell fresh and inviting and make you want to curl up in bed.

☐ **Keep your clothes under control**
The ultimate goal is to have fewer things. Shop smart, avoid impulse buys with The Saturday Test, find a rental service you love, and invest in a quality capsule wardrobe. Slow fashion down. Remember: something beautiful, something borrowed or something preloved can be even more stylish than something brand new.

☐ **Love your wardrobe**
Your clothes should make you smile every time you open the wardrobe, so take care of what you have. Review regularly (and recycle, donate or resell) to make sure you have long-lasting love for every item.

☐ **Seasonal storage solutions**
It's tricky to house a year's worth of clothes in one wardrobe. Rotate your pieces and remember to think practically about how regularly you'll need to access off-season items like winter coats or light summer trousers before you store them. If you have space in the loft or spare room, a rail with a rail protector is ideal.

☐ **Get the hang of it**
Hangers, baskets, drawer dividers and hanging rails... look at your wardrobe once you've had your big clear out and work out what you need to make it work beautifully for you. Always group by type and remember unless you have a huge walk-in wardrobe never arrange your entire wardrobe in blocks of colour – it will look a million dollars but you'll never find anything...

☐ **The art of accessorizing**
Keep your hats, belts, gloves and scarves sensibly stored in as few locations as possible. When deciding where to store your things, think whether you could put a stylish twist on your storage solution. Could you use an elegant jewellery stand or tree for your necklaces? Could you tie your collection of neck scarves onto a rail, hang them over ornate coat hooks or roll them beautifully in a basket? Simple, chic, cost-effective.

Bathroom

Bathrooms are so important because they are where we get fresh, prepare for the day ahead and wash away the stress before bed. A lot goes on in a bathroom, emotionally, too. It's the room where you might find out that you're pregnant or where you take a shower to improve your mood after getting bad news. If you've had a rough day at work, maybe you've wound up crying in the loo. Bathrooms are also the place we go for a sneaky snog at parties... I know I have!

As a teenager, the bathroom was somewhere I could go for a sneaky smoke. I was so desperate to smoke I would steal my dad's Hamlet cigars, nip in, shove a towel under the bathroom door and hang out of the window. Other than that, I didn't want to spend any time in there. It was a tiny room and although there wasn't any space to make a mess, everything was dated and the shower curtain smelled musty.

My mum and dad didn't have many products, but inside the bathroom cabinet and airing cupboard it was chaotic. There was a mismatch of scratchy towels, random linen and worn out sheets. Nothing felt clean and the whole space was claustrophobic. In comparison, the bathroom in the first house I rented with my husband, which was also tiny, was bright and light and everything was fresh.

We sometimes overlook this private, personal space and forget its importance. So much goes on in a bathroom, not just washing, so I want you to think about how your bathroom makes you feel. Is your bathroom somewhere you can light a candle and easily relax, or is it somewhere you just want to get in and out of as quickly as possible? Your bathroom should be a room that you really want to walk into. Even if you're just brushing your teeth, you can make the process enjoyable by having a beautiful place to do it, with all of the products organized and every shelf having a purpose.

You should always make sure you have enough storage and if you haven't, get some more! I'm so embarrassed about my current bathroom because it's cramped, dated and still to be decorated. It hasn't got all the storage it needs but I know how I'll do it when it's time. If you're a real beauty lover with lots of products, buy shelves for them. I love the look of glass shelves to display perfume bottles and attractive face creams. Floating shelves make everything look beautiful too. Just make sure the way you arrange your products looks pretty, not cramped.

The goal of this chapter is to make your bathroom feel like a relaxing spa.

Like we discussed in the bedroom chapter, we want to make your bathroom feel like it's part of a really chic hotel. Your bathroom version 2.0 will be a more streamlined, calm space. Back in the bedroom I told you how paperwork around your bed can affect your sleep and your sex life. Maybe you haven't realized the stress a messy bathroom can create either. Just making sure your bathroom cabinet is organized is a small action that can make a huge change. Organizing your bathroom properly will ensure getting ready in the morning is as smooth as it possibly can be so you can start your day feeling relaxed.

Have a Vision for the Bathroom

As I take you through each room in your house, I want you to identify why your space is cluttered. This book is far more than a collection of organizing hacks. What you'll learn is far deeper than a quick fix. You're gaining knowledge that will make you think about, and truly understand, why things are like this.

I want you to feel less defined by all the things in your home and break away from any labels you've picked up. Perhaps you've fallen into a rut of being 'the messy one', but you don't have to be. You just need to have vision.

Even if you think you're really disorganized and 'collect' clutter easily, the best way to change that is to bring your house back to its original state. How was it when you first moved in? Go back to how your bathroom was and think about how you wanted it to look, then ask yourself the questions at the bottom of page 51.

With the answers to those questions in mind, close your eyes and envision your bathroom as a blank space. Now ask yourself: how can I create the best version of my bathroom? How do I want to change it? Get a picture in your mind of what you want your bathroom to look like and then work at that. This is the best way to get yourself out of the rut of being suffocated by stuff.

Don't let the clutter around you define you or feel like it's your burden.

Look past all of the clutter to the end goal of what you want the space to look like, then keep going until you get there. Don't stop until your bathroom – and eventually your entire home! – is the ultimate version of what it could be. Then you can feel free of the stuff that is weighing you down and move beyond thinking you are 'the messy one'.

I cleaned out a loft last week. I decided how I wanted it to look and I didn't stop until it looked exactly like the image in my head. But perhaps you don't have a goal or a vision – that's OK! But in that case, I'd suggest you need the help of a professional organizer. There is no shame in asking for help when you feel overwhelmed by a situation. People ask for help to clean their houses, they ask for help with the ironing, you can get help with childcare... I need you to know that asking someone to help with your home is not being defeated, it's simply saying, 'I need help.' If you are feeling really overwhelmed, remember to imagine your room as a blank space and then plan how you would recreate that space if you could start again. You can.

Does This Space Make Me Feel Happy?

» Is my bathroom what I imagined it would be when I moved in?
» How are the products divided up in my bathroom cabinet?
» Are my shelves a mismatch of products or am I keeping my skincare stuff together, dental stuff together, etc.?
» Is my shower full of half-used shampoos, conditioners and body washes?
» Is my bath and shower hard to clean because it's so full of products?
» Would I feel happy for a guest to use my bathroom without hiding away excess products or wet towels first?
» Does this room help my morning routine run smoothly?
» Do I enjoy relaxing in here?

Edit Your Products

Share your beauty secrets

In your bathroom cabinet, all there should be are your daily essentials that you can access with ease. If you are a spender and constantly buying new products you need to ask yourself: why am I constantly buying new things? Is it because you feel you have problem skin? Are you always looking for a solution and the products you buy aren't working so you keep trying something else? Why do you feel the need to buy new products before the old ones have been used up? Dig a little deeper and consider whether you need professional advice. Perhaps you need to visit a dermatologist or take a trip to a beauty counter where the specialists really know their stuff. Go to an expert, share your skin concerns and ask for advice.

Invest in the best

Your skin is what everyone sees first so it's crucial you feel confident. If you are using the wrong products and you're constantly buying new things, you're probably buying them because you think they are going to make your skin better – but you might be making it worse. As well as expert advice, you should invest in quality products (and there are some brilliant

affordable products around). Always research what you are putting on your face and always patch test on first use.

In the same vein, spending money on a lovely hand wash, like one from Aesop, is a good investment. It will zhuzh up your bathroom and make you feel happy every time you wash your hands. It might seem like an unnecessary expense to spend money on soap you simply wash down the drain, but every hand wash will feel like a tiny pocket of happiness. I think that's worth the investment. My husband says candles are a waste of money because you are (almost literally) burning cash, and the same could be said of hand wash. You don't want the kids to splash it everywhere but if you can treat yourself to something special, it will add to the value of how you feel in a space.

Make small changes

When we get our bathrooms done up, we often buy a few pretty products and a candle and limit the items on display. That ups the emotional attachment we have to the space. But fast-forward a year and it's back to multi-buying, filling up the shelves with special offers and the clutter has returned. How was the room when you first moved in or redecorated? Go back to that vision. Remember, small changes make a big difference. If you took the tampons off the windowsill and hid the razors in a small box, your bathroom would look fresher again, wouldn't it? What about changing to a matching shampoo and conditioner so the shelves look neater? 'Edit out' the things that aren't attractive and only display beautiful things.

Shop smart

I've said it before (see page 14) and I'll say it a lot throughout this book: stop buying blind. Before you even think about going shopping you need to know what you already have in your house. The people I work with are forever buying blind! And bathroom products are one of the biggest temptations for this type of purchase.

One thing you absolutely have to remember is to use up your products before you go and buy something else. If you use a bit of your exfoliator and then get tempted by something new, you're just going to end up with overflowing cabinets and lots of half-used products,

way past their best. Using the very last drop before you replace something will slow down the cycle of overconsumption AND reduce the number of things you have cluttering up your cabinet. Stop buying blind and you'll shop smarter.

Save money

As well as bringing too much physical stuff into our houses, buying blind costs us a lot of money too. I want you to reduce the clutter in your home by having less stuff and save money because you only buy things you need. For instance, you might think you need a new moisturizer but actually, have you looked through your four drawers, two cabinets and that make-up bag of overflow beauty products? I bet there is one you have been gifted and never used already in there... somewhere. You just forgot about it because you can't get to your products. Or perhaps you've not had time to go through everything and as it's not laid out in front of you, it's out of sight and out of mind. Whether you need two products or ten products to get yourself ready, it's important to know exactly what you have, to have somewhere to store everything, and to keep it all organized properly.

How to Clean Up Your Bathroom

1 Reset the room
When you come to tackle your bathroom, dedicate a few hours to getting the job done. Make sure you have enough storage – think about baskets, hampers, clear containers, bathroom organizers and a shower caddy. Start by gutting the space entirely. Empty the cabinets, the windowsills, the shower and clear the shelves. Give everything a good deep clean and look at the space you have. Re-evaluate that space and really consider what you need to store. How can you make the space work for you? The goal is to make your bathroom look beautiful.

2 Gather and group
Once you know you have enough storage the most important thing is to gather your products together in groups – dental, bath and shower, skincare, medicines, etc. I'm sure you have products stashed all over the house. Check your bedroom dresser, your handbag and your car and then divide everything into groups. Have you got a dozen different bottles of shower gels, shampoos and conditioners? How much have you got compared to what you actually use?

Do an audit and admit what you really use compared to what you have. It really pays to be ruthless so ditch crusty old items, anything you don't use, products that don't suit your skin or duplicates. (See page 182 for information on donating new and unused duplicate products to beauty or hygiene banks.) Then it's back to the golden rule. Always use up what you have before you buy something else!

3 Zhuzh the space
Take your mind back to that feeling of organized space you envisioned when you moved in and then s-l-o-w-l-y start to add products back, keeping in mind you don't want to put everything out again. Don't pile stuff back on the windowsill. (I bet there are piles of products blocking the light there right now!) Could you add some plants or a scented candle instead to make the space look better?

4 Store products with purpose
Head to your bathroom cabinet and make sure every shelf has a purpose. If you open your bathroom cabinet and all sorts of products tumble out, you're going to waste time looking for things,

especially if you live with someone else. When someone else moves things around then puts them back in a different place – because they are looking for their products – life gets messy. If you both have products but you only have one bathroom cabinet, can you split the cabinet in two, so you both have a half? You'll have different things on each shelf but you both brush your teeth so dental products can be kept together.

Also think about the process you follow when you're getting ready and arrange items in your cabinet in the order you use them. For instance, start by finding a place for your cleanser, because that's what you use first thing, followed by toner. Moisturizer goes on the next shelf up. Keep one make-up bag for daily use then store the overflow, nicely arranged, somewhere else so you aren't scrambling around looking for everything all the time. Maybe you're into your brands so one shelf has all your Chanel products and another is full of Bobbi Brown. Use containers inside your bathroom cabinet to group your products, which you can then label.

5 Tackle the towels

Bring structure into your airing cupboard. Being organized means everything can be easily accessed so keep your bath towels together, your bath mats together and facecloths all together. If you don't have an airing cupboard, you could roll your towels and keep them neatly stored in baskets or hampers. I always advise investing in the best towels you can afford – they'll stay softer for longer.

So how many towels do you actually have? I really think you only need three towels per person. One to use, one in the wash and one spare. Keep them on rotation and you really don't need more than that. For more advice, see page 87.

It's a lot easier to organize your bathroom – and keep it organized – if you have less stuff in the first place. Once your space is minimal, clean and calm, you'll find it so much easier to relax.

›› Your Bathroom and Beauty Products

First group all your products together by type – your shampoos, conditioners, cleansers and dental kit. Edit out anything you don't use, products that don't suit your skin or duplicates. (For information on donating new and unused duplicate products, see page 182.)

›› The Bathroom Windowsill

Move any random bottles or items from the windowsill so that area is fresh and clear. Perhaps you've got some houseplants that are in the front room? Move them onto the windowsill to create a calmer, more relaxing space.

›› The Medicine Cabinet

It's so important to store your medicines safely and tidily. Start by emptying out the containers you use now then group all the children's medicines together, put painkillers together, store first-aid items with each other, then group prescriptions. If you can dedicate a whole shelf to medicines you could have six or so containers to keep everything separate. Then it will be really easy for you to grab your supplements or vitamins – or to have speedy access to the first-aid kit if there is a cut or a graze that needs to be seen to.

A word on safety: children's medicines should always be kept separate from adult medicines and the latter should be in a separate, locked box somewhere out of sight. It's so important to make sure that there is no way your children could ever get hold of potentially dangerous adult items. Think about the positioning of your medicine cabinet or box. Mine is on a high shelf in the hall. Whether you keep yours in the bathroom, utility room or in the hall like me, I really recommend you keep it somewhere high up and out of the reach of children.

Dolly Dash

Bathroom Checklist

CLEAN UP YOUR BATHROOM AND WASH YOUR TROUBLES AWAY

☐ **Get a fresh perspective**
When we're surrounded by stuff, it's hard to see how things can get better. So imagine what your bathroom would look like if it was completely empty and give yourself – and the space – a clean slate. You don't have to be 'the messy one' or have a messy bathroom. Think about how you can make things more organized and tranquil, then set to work on realizing that vision in your space. Do not stop until you achieve your goal.

☐ **Take a spa break**
It's amazing how small changes make such a big difference. A few little luxuries will help you enjoy a spa-like experience every day and fill the room with pockets of happiness. Think about adding a candle with a relaxing fragrance, a plant for greenery, or a beautifully scented hand wash.

☐ **Pick your products carefully**
If your bathroom is full of half-used beauty and bath products you need to slow down. To feel confident in our own skin we need to feel confident in the products we choose for it. So ask for expert advice, invest in fewer, better products, finish every last drop before you buy more and never buy blind. Your skin will glow, and you'll save time, money and space – that's the beauty of it.

☐ **Routine check your bathroom cabinet**
To save time and start the day stress free, check that your bathroom cabinet mirrors your morning routine. From contact lenses to skincare, and dental products to grooming, make sure every shelf has a purpose.

☐ **Throw in your towels**
It's also a good idea to regularly check your bath linen. Never store more than three towels per person and only keep the best. (See page 87 for more advice.)

Kitchen

Kitchens are my favourite room in the house to organize because they are such a powerful space in our homes. I love them above everything else because they can make such a difference to people's lives. They are totally functional but they are also the hub of the house. Kitchens shape the way we interact with our families and the memories we create together, so we really need to take the time to look after them...

That's a lesson I learned from my childhood. Growing up, my kitchen was the only room in the house that was cleaned daily. Every morning when I came downstairs, the kitchen was always tidy. Even now, before I go to bed, I always make sure my kitchen is clean... unless I am very, very drunk! Seeing greasy pans in the sink from the night before is so depressing. At home, the washing up always had to be done before bed. We had a really tiny galley kitchen but we did have a pantry, although this was always full to the brim and always cluttered! At the bottom there were bottles of soft drinks, then breads and cereals were on the next shelf up. There was some kind of organization system but all in all, it was pretty dark and disorderly.

The galley part was full of cupboards with laminate doors in a beige colour with a lip to open them. It's so strange, I can remember every detail about those cupboards so clearly. I also vividly remember my dad sitting on a funny little stool in the kitchen eating banana on toast (it was the only thing he could make himself) with a mug of tea. Dad was a big man and the stool was tiny! I've still got his mug, it's the only one I kept. It was my dad who taught me that the kitchen has to be clean before you go to bed. The kitchen was also where my mum taught me to make Sri Lankan food and I remember eating out of the pan while she was cooking... and in fact, I still do that to this day!

There are so many lovely things that the kitchen reminds me of – it was always a very happy and positive place.

When we look back at how we used kitchens in the past, they were often purely functional spaces. Now when you go to view a house all you can think is, 'How can I make this kitchen bigger? How can I open it up?' It's such an important room and we all desire to make it a cooking, eating and social space. When I was little, our neighbours had the dream kitchen. It was big and open-plan with a huge table that you could sit at, eat at and see everyone. Their house was the vision of what I wanted my home to be like when I was older and now my kitchen, as everyone knows, is the most important room in my house.

I want my kitchen to be an organized and inviting place. Everything I do in terms of design involves thinking about our family and friends. That's the feeling our home creates. It's a party house, a fun house and it's definitely not a show house. I want it to be a space where you feel relaxed. I want people to walk through that front door, sit at the table and feel like they've been here forever!

Create a Kitchen That Flows

This is one of the biggest chapters of the book because organizing a kitchen is a large job. Kitchens are where we start our day, where the family congregates and where we share a few words before we all go off on our journeys to work or school.

If the kitchen is always cluttered and chaotic, it's not going to support the start of our day or allow us to relax and enjoy the time we get to spend together Think how your space feels right now and ask yourself the questions at the bottom of page 63.

When I talk about the 'flow' of your kitchen, I want to know how easily you move from one task to the next. For instance, how smoothly can you move from ingredient prep, to finding the equipment you need to cook, to pulling out a dish to serve the finished meal.

The goal is the make things as easy and efficient as possible. The simplest way to create flow without bringing in the builders is to zone your space by function, for example, cleaning, food prep, cooking and so on. (For more tips and advice on zoning spaces see page 75.) You could also consider creating a 'breakfast zone' (with the toaster, coffee maker and all your breakfast supplies) to help the morning routine run like clockwork.

It's essential that your kitchen flows and has a structure that works for the whole household.

If you have kids, think about whether they can access their breakfast stuff. Can they get their own plates and bowls? How are you teaching your children to access their things? Can they lay the table themselves? Or do you have to do everything for them because everything is stored up high? If your kids are at the age when they can take responsibility for laying the table, you could create a kids' drawer or a breakfast drawer for the whole family. Every morning you can all muck in together because everyone knows where the breakfast things are stored – and everyone can reach them.

Organizing the kitchen is a big job. If you are not in a good place mentally, your home won't be in a good place. Even with the best will in the world, decluttering won't help you out. So firstly you need to work out whether you are happy in your home. Ask yourself:

» Are you really ready to begin?
» If you're not ready, why is that?
» Can you address any of those issues now?
» Do you need professional help?

For more information and support, see pages 180–181.

Does This Space Make Me Feel Happy?

» Is my kitchen what I imagined it would be when I moved in?
» Is it impossible to find the ingredients I need because the cupboards are so overcrowded?
» Is the sink or dishwasher constantly full of dishes?
» Are the counters too cluttered for food prep?
» Do I enjoy cooking and/or eating in this space?
» When I come downstairs in the morning, does the kitchen help my morning routine run smoothly?
» Can I find everything easily?
» Can I get to the breakfast items easily?
» Does my kitchen flow?

A TALE OF CHAOS TO CALM

Lighter and brighter

'We had a beautiful kitchen and yet I didn't enjoy it. It was chaotic and mixed up: we had smoked paprika in three different places, peanut butter in the smoothie section and in the breakfast drawer with the spreads, the list went on and on... The flow of the room wasn't working. I felt overwhelmed and frustrated in the space. I didn't know how to sort it out as there was so much stuff and a lot of it was other people's as I live in a large extended family.

Dilly helped so much! First she took everything out of the cupboards, which I would never have had the courage to do! She then looked at the flow of the kitchen and reorganized it to make it make more sense. For instance, Dilly put the tea stuff near the hot water tap, and moved our glasses away from the kitchen table and into a cupboard near the sink. She used baskets, dividers and, best of all, a labelling machine – not only to transform the kitchen but to ensure it was easy for us to maintain the structure and keep it organized. Dilly was so kind and walked through the whole house to give me tips on how to tackle other areas myself. She is the loveliest lady and doesn't judge. She is passionate about helping you enjoy your space. Dilly also has serious stamina and doesn't stop – she just powers through!

I feel like I've taken off a heavy backpack! I literally feel lighter on my feet! We waste much less now as we can see where everything is, so we know what needs to be used up and don't buy more than we need. The kitchen is my favourite place to sit now and I'm cooking more than ever!'

A TALE OF CHAOS TO CALM

A Dolly for life

'From the outside our kitchen looked great. When you opened a drawer it was a different story... Stuff seemed to be everywhere. We were forever opening cupboards to search for the things we needed and the space felt disjointed. I was anxious whenever we had guests round – they would comment on the lovely kitchen then look in a drawer and see a disaster zone. Dilly completely rejigged the layout, which now really flows. We blitzed the room and decided what we really needed. We grouped all the hot drink making items together – it sounds so simple but I had things in different cupboards. We put the cereal in see-through containers so the children can help themselves. Their items are grouped together now too, which makes the kids so much more independent. Anything used once a year was put in one place so we have space for the things we use every day. Dilly also suggested bamboo containers (amongst others) and some amazing cutlery dividers.

Our kitchen has a completely different vibe now. I'm happy for anyone to look around without having to shout, 'That's the junk drawer!' It sounds crazy that a messy kitchen can cause anxiety but the feeling in a decluttered kitchen is one of peace and harmony. I know it sounds super-melodramatic but it's made a huge change in our house. I love entertaining again and don't feel embarrassed. The best thing is definitely our food organization. Our pasta, cereals, tins, and so on, are all organized – we no longer overbuy because we can see the back of the cupboards. Everything Dilly implemented has stuck and in most cases developed into habit for the whole family – we all refill the jars and the kids tell me when the cereal container is nearly empty rather than leaving an empty box on the shelf. It really made me want to sort other areas in my house that were overflowing, especially the bathroom cabinet and my make-up! I'm a converted Dolly for life.'

Use Containers to Control Your Spending

Check your cupboards

Once again, the key to reducing the chaos in your kitchen cupboards is to shop smarter, never buy blind and always know what you already have before you go shopping. You have 15 different types of pasta – all in half-empty bags – because you often go to the supermarket vaguely thinking you need pasta. But if you had checked your cupboards, if you could actually get to the back of your shelves, you would have realized you absolutely did not need any more pasta.

Every time you go shopping you keep repeating that process because you never look... you never check... and you will never truly know what you have until you've pulled everything out and gone through all the packets.

Pretty practical

Containers are not just an aesthetic storage solution, they allow us to understand when we need more. When you choose one brand of pasta and put it in a container, you can instantly see when it's half-full and when it's time for a top-up. The reason we put things in containers is so we can see exactly what we have and can identify when we need to buy more, so we can control our spending. Kilner jars work particularly well – they look smart, keep the food fresh and, crucially, allow you to see in an instant what you have. Most of us are creatures of habit when it comes to dry goods and we pick the same type of rice, same shape of pasta and so on. So if you can find a brand you like, stick to it, store it in a container and never buy blind.

Group your goods

Everything in your kitchen cupboards should have its own place with everything kept together by type. So group together your dry goods, your spices, your condiments and so on, so you can see exactly what you have.

Think of your cleaning products... if the cloths are spread over four or five cupboards with some under the kitchen sink, some in the utility room and some in the bathroom, how can you possibly know how many cloths you have? So you go out and buy more... It's the same with the grocery shop. If everything in your food cupboards is accessible and you can see what you have at a glance, your shopping list will be shorter and you'll save money on your weekly shop.

Reduce your food waste

Often we have those 15 half-eaten bags of pasta in our cupboards because we haven't used up what we already had. So before you try a new brand or a new type of product – whether that's pasta, lentils or biscuits – eat what's in your cupboards first. You'll reduce your food waste and save money.

More often than not, cereal is the biggest culprit for not getting used up. So many families have dozens of boxes of cereal in their cupboards. Why? Because the kids are pestering you to try a different variety! If you don't make your children finish what they have before they move onto the next thing, the cupboards are going to get more and more cluttered. We need to instil discipline in our children – and ourselves. If we want to try something new, we have to finish what we have already. (For tips on combating food waste see page 68.)

When you tackle the kitchen, it's likely you'll discover products that need to be thrown away. Food waste is bad for the environment and bad for your bank balance. The guilt of throwing food away also makes us feel bad. Here are a few ways to combat food waste:

» Recycle items past their use by date. Please don't eat items that are past their use by date. Even if the item looks – and smells – OK, it could pose a health risk. Instead, see if the item could be added to your council food waste bin or to your compost bin so your garden can benefit. Thoroughly clean any packaging so it's ready to be recycled.

» With best before dates it's best to use common sense. If the item is only just past its best, use your judgement. Could you make a particular dish to use it up quickly? If you're in any doubt, deal with the item as above.

» Share your food. If you have items you've tried and weren't for you, don't leave them on the shelf. Would work colleagues love those cookies you found too sweet? Would your brother enjoy that sauce that wasn't spicy enough? Ask around before you throw things away but never offload items onto others unless they are wanted.

» Don't be eaten up by guilt. Organizing your kitchen will help you keep waste to a minimum moving forwards. If you stop buying blind, you'll never buy more than you need.

» Donate instead of waste. Consider picking up an extra item each time you shop – or whenever you can – to donate to your local food bank.

Organize Your Fridge and Freezer

Game-changing containers

As well as Kilner jars in the cupboards, I keep containers in the fridge. My husband hates having containers in the fridge but I really freak out if there aren't any. Last year I had some containers, which had been gifted and labelled beautifully, but they melted in the dishwasher and I had to recycle them. While I was waiting for the new ones to arrive, I felt beyond stressed. I couldn't control the fridge as I had no way of putting it in order so everything was just getting piled in.

Containers are game-changers – the beauty of them is that they give structure to our fridges and divide each shelf in half. Each half has a section and each section has a purpose. Keep your dairy together, store the vegetables together, meats together, salads, cheeses... If you can add a lazy Susan for your condiments, you won't have to reach over items to get to the back of the shelf either. And you can always see if there is any mint sauce left before you head out and buy more.

Love labels

When I was little, we did a holiday swap with an American family and I clearly remember my mum had put a label in the fridge where the freshest milk should go: 'Please use the milk from this end.' That label stayed there for most of my childhood. I still love a label in the fridge! I also label everything in my freezer.

Freezer sections

I know that not everyone has a big freezer but if you can section off your freezer, absolutely do it, otherwise it will become a big void. Upright freezers are the most versatile, so if you're designing a new kitchen try to add that into your design. I hate chest freezers! They are so hard to organize – unless you have storage boxes inside them. I like the stackable sort that can store all your food in sections (see page 187).

Whatever size and shape your freezer is, always label the drawers and add containers. Keep your pizzas together, breads together, peas, chips, ice-cream and everything else all together in their sections. Everything needs a drawer and every drawer should be divided. Watch out if anyone tries to mess up those sections in my house – although that happens often!

Reduce
Your
Counter
Clutter

Attack of the appliances

Most of the houses I visit have an overload of appliances. Have a look at your worktops now... Is there a radio, microwave, pasta maker, food processor? There are so many different gadgets people keep in their homes that are kept out all year long, but I bet the majority will only be used once or twice a year. Yet they are still sat on the kitchen surfaces gathering dust.

I want to help you reduce the amount of stuff on your worktops so think about what appliances you have and how often you use them. If the only items you use on a daily basis are the toaster and kettle, they are the only things that need to be on your counter. You might not even eat toast every morning so perhaps your toaster could be hidden away and only brought out on weekends? With everything on your worktops, think about whether each item really earns its place on the counter.

Style and sense

Once you only have the items you use on a daily basis, think about how they look. Are they aesthetically pleasing? Are they purposeful? How could you create more space? Consider the size of your fruit bowl... count up the vases you have... look at the colour of your appliances... All these things matter hugely!

You might have a dark grey kettle, a dark grey toaster and a dark grey microwave. These three heavy grey units on a white counter top might make the space look heavy. If you swap them for white appliances, your counter is suddenly going to look a lot lighter and brighter. I actually think microwaves are a dying breed. What do you use your microwave for? If you only use it to defrost things, can you plan ahead instead and decide on tomorrow's dinner tonight? Then you can get the chicken out the freezer, let it defrost in the fridge and lose the bulky microwave. Likewise, if you're only using the microwave to reheat a tin of beans, donate or recycle it and use the hob instead. Look at the products you use and decide if they make sense for the space.

If you love music in the kitchen but have a big old hi-fi taking up space, do you swap it for a tiny little smart speaker or something streamlined? Is your windowsill cluttered with a dozen different plants? It's lovely to have plants on your windowsill but if you can't see out of the window and the plants are blocking the light and making the kitchen feel dark, you should move them out.

If you're at the point at which you can barely prepare a meal on your worktops – and I've seen this in many houses – you have to change things up. Get rid of the paperwork and lose the cluttered utensil pot (which you only use one spoon from anyway). Only keep the bare minimum – the things you really need – on your counters.

How to Organize Your Kitchen

1 Do your prep properly
Start with proper preparation. When you've decided to tidy the room, begin your planning a few days before. Get everything you may need together. Have enough containers and drawer dividers to hand (see pages 186–187 for more advice). Give yourself plenty of time and block out a whole day where you can tidy uninterrupted. Devote at least 6–8 hours to a kitchen. I might be able to organize a kitchen in 4–6 hours but I know exactly what I'm doing and won't find it as stressful as you will because it's not my kitchen. I can come into your house with purpose but it's a very different scenario when it's your own home!

2 Reset the room
Whack on some tunes and clean the kitchen floor. Next empty every single cupboard, drawer and shelf into the middle of the floor then clean the sides, surfaces, windowsills... Clear it all and clean the space thoroughly. You have to pull everything out or you'll end up trying to tidy on top of things. One of the most important lessons in this book is that if you want to organize any space, you need to gut the area or you're not going to see the potential and possibilities it has to offer. Plus, when it's time to add things back into the empty space you'll be inspired to keep it clear because it will look so spacious and fresh.

3 Check and collect
With all the things you now have in the middle of your floor, group them all. Match up all the Tupperware with their lids. Put all the glassware together, group the Pyrex dishes, the ceramics, serving dishes, pots and pans... Everything should be collected in its type. Next check all your produce for dates and if there is out-of-date food, get rid of it responsibly (see page 68 for tips).

4 The cupboards are bare...

... and with a blank space in front of you, you can, at last, see the kitchen properly and can identify what works best. It's only when it's empty that you are able to look at things differently. When your eyes see cupboards that are full of a mismatch of stuff, it's impossible for your brain to make sense of the space.

So look at your empty cupboards. Did the previous contents really work best in that position? Could they be better somewhere else? Did your kitchen flow before? Think about how you can make it better. Could you create zones for cleaning, food prep and cooking? (See page 75.) Could you switch up the cupboards and make a dedicated space for all your glasses and drinks – rather than having an amalgamation of spices, baking bowls and tin cans? Maybe there really is nowhere else to move the plates to, but you can definitely make them look neater. Ask yourself: am I making the most of the space?

5 Soup up your storage

It's really important to maximize your storage space. Use every inch of your kitchen and if you have a small kitchen, it's even more vital to use the space properly. So many people move into a house and put things in cupboards but never change how they unpacked.

Try moving the shelves to different heights to make better use of the space. When I go round to people's houses, I'll point out things that don't fit and ask if they've tried moving the shelf? It's so simple but no-one ever thinks of it! To make your kitchen work for you, you must make the available space work for you.

6 Clear out to clean up

When you have a plan and know what you want to store where, go through all your items. Decide what you want to keep and be ruthless. When did you last use it? Why are you keeping it? Is it sentimental or for expense? Is it really a valid reason?

Check your multiples. If you have several of something, only keep the best. You don't need seven corkscrews or five potato peelers! (See page 99 for advice on editing down your dinnerware.) Cutlery drawers are a mess magnet. I know if you have kids you keep medicine syringes in there – everyone keeps them in their cutlery drawer. Everyone has chopsticks from the takeaway that are still in their paper wrappers too. And that's just the tip of the iceberg – people keep the craziest stuff in their cutlery drawer. It's time to clear it out.

As you go through the cleansing process, put your excess items into piles for keeping, donating, recycling and rubbish. Remember, when you put things back, always do so in groups. All the mugs together, glasses together, the mixing bowls together... There shouldn't be any random items in your cupboards.

Now that every drawer, shelf and cupboard has a purpose you need to stick to that moving forwards. Everything I discuss in this book is completely achievable – you just need to work out the best way to make this advice work for you. By the time you've finished, you'll have a kitchen that flows and a beautiful space for the whole family to enjoy.

Zoning Spaces 101

In the same way it's helpful to group items by type (your dry goods, your cleaning products, your skincare), it helps the flow of a room to zone spaces by function. This is particularly key in the kitchen and utility room where practicality is so important. Every room is different, but here are some suggestions for zones you could create in your space.

KITCHEN ZONES

Dishes if you can store all of your dinnerware (plates, bowls, glasses, cutlery, etc.) near the dishwasher or the sink, the task of tidying everything away will be easier and faster – even if it still isn't much fun...

Food prep you could make that meal in 15 minutes if your mixing bowls, chopping boards, knives and peeler are ready for action near your main work surface (it also helps for them to be close to the sink for speedy cleaning).

Cooking if you can keep your essential utensils, pots, pans, baking trays and the ingredients you cook with regularly (oils, spices, seasonings, etc.) close to the cooker, you'll always be cool and calm when following a recipe.

Breakfast if you're really in the zone(!), set up an area with the toaster, kettle, coffee machine, tea bags, coffee beans, cereals, etc., all close at hand, so you'll always have time for breakfast.

UTILITY ZONES

Laundry and cleaning few people love doing laundry, but if you keep your products, dryers and ironing equipment in one spot near your washer and dryer (if you have one), your sorting and folding will be sorted. Likewise, if you keep all your cleaning products and equipment together, grouped by room (see page 84), it will be simple for everyone to find them so they can easily help with the chores – and deal with stains at speed!

The Fridge

Empty the fridge completely, wipe down every shelf to make it fresh and clean. When you bring the items back, make sure to keep all your dairy products together, all your fish together, all the ready meals together, all the vegetables together, the condiments together... It will really help you if you can keep the types of foods separate (as well as being important for food safety to keep your raw meats away from cooked items). To add essential structure, you could bring in extra containers or even a lazy Susan and store your table sauces on it. You'll never have to scramble around the back of the fridge to find the mustard again!

Your Spices

You can Dolly Dash your spices and create a spice drawer really quickly and easily. I like to group my spices by brand because it looks neater. You can decant your spices into the same type of container or only buy the same brand of spice if you don't want to decant. Instantly your spice drawer will look better. Once all the spices are in the same jars, I arrange them alphabetically. This way, when you scan the spices you will find the one you're looking for much more quickly.

Tupperware

Wherever you keep your Tupperware, empty the area completely and then find all the random tubs you might have scattered around the house. Make sure that every lid has a matching bottom and try to avoid storing the lids away from their bases. Keeping them separate will mean you spend ages searching for a matching set when you need to use it. Then, stack the tubs from biggest to smallest and, where possible, put the smaller sets inside the larger ones. If you have any excess containers that have lost a lid, don't get rid of them – use them for lining your drawers to organize your stationery or make-up.

Dolly Dash

Kitchen Checklist

CLEAR OUT AND COOK UP AN ORGANIZED, SOCIAL SPACE

☐ **Go with the flow**
Tackling the kitchen is a big job but if you can add structure and create a kitchen that flows, you'll find you have more space (and feel less stressed) when performing any kitchen task – from making a cup of tea to preparing dinner for four.

☐ **Contain yourself**
The fridge, freezer and cupboards can quickly get out of control, but if we stop buying blind, stick to one brand at a time, use up every last crumb before buying more, and store our goods in containers, we can control our spending and minimize our food waste. It's a no-brainer.

☐ **Smarten up your storage**
Smart storage solutions will help bring order to a chaotic kitchen. Think about adding Kilner jars to the cupboards, containers to your fridge and freezer or even a lazy Susan to help you keep an eye on your condiments.

☐ **Clean up your counters**
It's so easy for clutter to build up on your work surfaces – from unopened post and rows of plant pots to that barely used pasta maker. If there's no space left to prepare your evening meal, it's time to have a clear-out. Sort and recycle the paperwork and re-home the plants. Carefully edit your appliances – would it be better to donate that slow cooker and buy a kettle that matches the toaster so your surfaces feel considered and less busy? Keep the bare minimum on your work surfaces for maximum productivity in the kitchen.

☐ **Never go to bed with a messy kitchen**
It's a small takeaway from this chapter, but it's a priceless piece of advice that I still live by today. You'll always be happy to wake up to a clean kitchen.

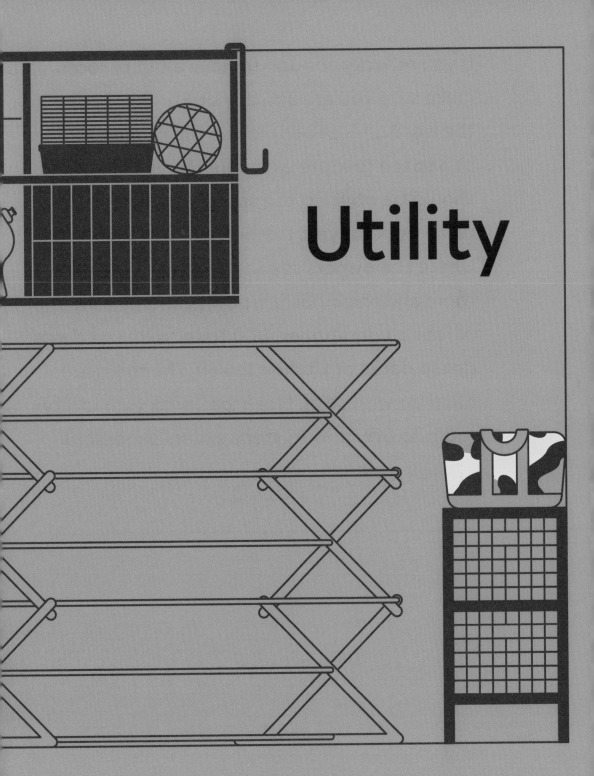

Utility

If you're lucky enough to have a utility room, make sure you are actually utilizing it. Look at the word... Most people use their utility room as a space to store extra bulk buys but you should be *utilizing* the space and making it really work for you. I've been in so many houses where the owners see the space in a utility room and think, 'Great, now I can buy 6 litres of fabric conditioner, 800 toilet rolls and three dozen packs of kitchen towel!' The room is filled up with stuff. No! Stop using your utility room as overflow to store excess shopping!

My childhood home didn't have the luxury of a utility room but the home of my next door neighbours (who I adored) did have one. I thought it was genius that they had created this separate space to do all the washing and dry their clothes! Seeing their utility room made me decide that I wanted one when I grew up... it was my dream! I can't remember whether they had an integrated clothes dryer (also the dream), but what they did have was a sliding door so everything was hidden out of sight. (This was the early nineties and I know we all aspire to bi-fold doors nowadays, but then a sliding door was such a trendy thing to have.) My neighbour was a builder and the house was always full of the newest things. I thought they were so, so cool for having a utility room.

Like every room, you need to make sure it really works for you, so bring in a rail where you can hang and air your clothes. Ensure there is enough cupboard space to store your laundry, washing and cleaning products (but not in excessive quantities). Perhaps you need to carve out space for the kids' football boots, an area for pet items, or one for light bulbs and batteries. Do you need to store coats and wellies in here? Whatever you need, as usual, keep everything in groups by type. So make one space for your DIY kit, and another for medicines (if this is where you keep them). You need to make sure every single cupboard and shelf has structure and you need to view your kitchen and utility as separate rooms (or spaces) with very different purposes. Let's make a clean sweep of it.

Your utility room should be where you do practical things, like hang the washing on wet days, store light bulbs and do the laundry.

Create Space with Purpose

When you organized your kitchen, you might have moved random, non-food related items to the utility room – but don't treat it like an overflow kitchen. Never store excess kitchen products in your utility room. If you're following the principles of smart shopping (not buying blind and using up what you have before you buy more) there shouldn't be any extra stuff to store in there anyway! If you really do have masses of space in your house, you could use your utility for *some* storage, but one of the main reasons we organize is to control our spending.

Often when I visit one-bedroom flats in London there might just be a cupboard under the sink to create a utility area. So many people say, 'I don't have any space,' but when I look in that cupboard, they've got 48 toilet rolls and a stack of 25 rolls of kitchen towels! Why have you got all this stuff when there is only one person living in this flat?! We all have to live in the space we have, not the space we are dreaming of.

When people think they have space, they tend to go crazy and fill it with things they don't need. Using your utility room

as a storage facility is as wrong as using your garage to store 38 bottles of Diet Coke that you only bought because they were on offer... It's ridiculous the way some people fill their houses.

I know that utility rooms are a luxury and not everyone has a whole room, but whatever size house you have, and even if you have a tiny cupboard or shelf for your utility items, you still need to organize it correctly, give the space purpose and make it work hard for you. As with every room in the house, the only way to recreate that area is to imagine the space as if you've just moved in. If you look at your utility room right now, ignore all the stuff and imagine that the space is completely empty, then ask yourself the questions at the bottom of page 83.

Our homes are not storage spaces, they are living spaces.

It's key that we treat the utility area like living space. What you *need* to store is a good place to start when it comes to creating a space with purpose, as once you've made a list of the items that should be stored in the utility room, you can create storage that will allow you to utilize those items effectively. So what's on your list? Consider cleaning, laundry, recycling and pet items – and perhaps even your wellies. Zoning the space can help add purpose too (see page 75).

There can be surprise storage opportunities all around the house that you might never have thought of! Where can you add hooks to take things off the floor? Are there pegs on the back of your doors? Can you add shelving in your kitchen or dining room to create space for glassware? Are you using every possible inch of your home effectively? If you are, you'll have created the illusion of space while reducing clutter. Don't forget to look up, too. If you have a small kitchen you might want to add a hanging system for pots and pans.

Can you add laundry racks or slimline shoe storage to your utility room? There might be an area you can add some skinny shelves to. Shelves can make the biggest difference in the smallest of spaces. I organized a very small one-bedroom flat, which had a very clever, narrow shelving unit along the wall. Kilner jars sat on the shelves with various contents and although they hung over the shelf by a tiny, tiny amount, it was certainly not enough to topple them. Those shelves were such an effective use of space because they housed 40 jars of dry goods, freeing up space elsewhere.

Am I Happy With This Space?

> » Is the utility space as helpful as I thought it would be when I moved in?
> » Has it become a storage space?
> » Is there room to dry the laundry in here? Could there be?
> » What would I do differently if I started from scratch?
> » Would I move the cleaning products?
> » Would I put the cleaning cloths and equipment somewhere else?
> » Would I change that cabinet?
> » Would I use the surfaces differently?
> » Am I using the space effectively?
> » What do I actually need to store in here?

Sort Out Your Cleaning Products

Group by room

When you organize a utility space, try to separate all your cleaning products into their destinations – so keep them in an area for bathrooms, for kitchens, for polishes and one for random cleaning items. Grouping things makes it easier when you come to do the cleaning, or if your cleaner does it. As with every area we organize, we are doing it for a simpler life overall. Make it easy for whoever is doing the cleaning to get to everything they require in one go (you could even invest in a caddy). Once you have your items in groups, label them so everyone knows where things should go back – and then you can all find them easily again next time.

Deep cleaning

I use a Kärcher steam cleaner for everything. I deep clean my kitchen with it once a week and my kitchen sparkles! But I also use it on mirrors, windows and work surfaces.

Don't believe the hype

So often we are enticed by advertising and think, 'This will change my life!' Of course it doesn't, so the half-full bottle stays in the cupboard and you go and buy something else with a life-changing promise. If you do want to try a new product, don't buy anything until you have used what you already have! I recommend that once you've found a product that you like, stick to it. There are probably only 4–5 different types of surface in your house and you should know what works by now.

The fab five

Sometimes I discover a whole shop's worth of products under the sink when I'm organizing, but for a whole house you probably only need a handful of products to keep it clean. Here are my top five...

1. **Antibacterial spray** is important for your kitchen surfaces and cupboards
2. **Bleach** to disinfect and kill germs
3. **Bathroom cleaner** will keep things squeaky clean
4. **Limescale remover** is essential if you live in a hard water area
5. **Fairy liquid or Dawn** does the job for most things! It gets dirty marks off sofas, walls... even radiators

Most of the best professional cleaners only use four or five cleaning products. They even clean whole hotels with the bare minimum of product (plus a vacuum cleaner and a duster). Housekeeping will usually use two spray bottles. They will have an anti-bac in one bottle and some sort of limescale remover in the other.

#6 the secret superhero

I really don't believe you need lots of cleaning products when hot water and soap work so well, particularly when cleaning the kitchen. But polish is vital if you have lots of wood furniture. It's the perfect finishing touch for your surfaces, to make them shine and to give your room that fresh, clean smell.

Lucky #7

My under-the-sink stash is really minimal. I have the 'fab five' products, a can of furniture polish and, finally, some Flash for my floors. And that is it! Hot water and a microfibre cloth does everything else.

Nobody likes cleaning so most of the time we just give our homes a quick once-over and even if you are planning a deep clean, you won't need to use more than the products you already have. It's really important that you don't stockpile cleaning products to keep a clear space and clear mind.

How to Rework Your Utility

1 Make some space
If you don't have a utility room, a clever way of making a utility space is in the airing cupboard. Stack a washing machine and tumble drier above each other and then you'll have a slim space down the side or a gap for a little shelf.

2 Embrace minimalism
All you really need is one bottle of fabric conditioner, one packet of washing powder, three towels per person (see page 87) and a couple of bedsheets (one in use and one ready to go). Train yourself to stop buying in bulk and just keep one of everything. Keep it minimal.

3 Get inspired
People often find utility rooms hard to tackle as they feel uninspired by the space. If you're finding it tough, go on Pinterest and look for spaces similar to your own. Type in 'utility room storage' or 'laundry room ideas', 'utility cupboard', 'storage ideas', 'storage saving tips' or 'Ikea hacks'. It's brilliant for space-saving tips, so think about your storage and how you can make it Pinterest-worthy.

4 Reset and reimagine
Empty every cupboard, drawer and shelf and clean the space. What do you need to do to make this a space you can truly utilize – without changing the actual shell? Consider the gadgets and gizmos you could add. What about hooks or under-cabinet storage? Do you need new storage containers or glass jars? Look at the cupboards in a different light – repurpose them. So often I find people don't actually need to add anything to a room, they just need to readjust what they already have. You can add slim storage on the inside of the cupboard doors or use a lazy Susan to get to out-of-reach items. Alternatively, why not add baskets or false shelves. And don't forget to look up. You could hang a laundry airer from the ceiling to maximize your space.

Now you can see your utility space with a new perspective, know what items you need to store and have decided how you want it to look, you just have to keep going until you get there! For advice on zoning spaces, see page 75, or for advice on storage solutions see pages 186–187.

Love Your Linen 101

BEAUTIFUL BED LINEN

Stop keeping linen you've had since uni. When I go into houses, I see so much tatty linen and it won't make you want to cozy up in that bed every night or help you have a restful night's sleep.

Your bed is so important and so are your bedsheets! Make sure you update your pillows, sheets and duvets every year. And then recycle the old bedlinen. Go through every sheet you have and make sure you are keeping your sets together. I always keep the duvet cover, pillowcases, flat sheet and a bottom sheet tucked into one pillowcase. When it comes to changing the bed, you just grab one complete set and go! It's life-changing not to be scrabbling round looking for pillowcases and a matching bottom sheet. (See page 27 for more advice on beautiful bedding.)

SUPER-SOFT TOWELS

Getting dry with the 'help' of a threadbare old towel is depressing. Always go through your towels regularly to make sure you only have three really lovely towels per person, instead of 15 to 20 towels that are slightly stained with hair dye, because I know that's what is lurking in your laundry cupboard right now! Like everything in your house, you need to keep revisiting, recycling and refreshing because things become old very quickly.

When you do your laundry, make sure you wash and dry your towels properly. If you don't you could end up with hard, crispy towels, which are horrible and certainly don't improve the bathing experience. Always look after what you have.
If you have the space and can have a separate tumble dryer it means you will always have lovely fluffy towels that will make bath time such a pleasure. I know a lot of people simply don't have space for both machines but perhaps you might like to think about investing in a combi washer-dryer in the future.

The Recycling

The best way to keep your recycling ordered is to invest in a good recycling divider which will make it easy for you to throw your glass, plastic and cardboard in separately, if that is what is required in your area. It's important to develop good habits when it comes to recycling, so why not schedule this Dolly Dash for the same time every week – perhaps on your way to the supermarket. Alternatively, teach the kids about recycling by getting them involved in the dash before they head out to school. Make sure your items are separated as required and keep up to speed with what can and can't be recycled (the website of your local council or recycling centre should have all the information you need).

Pet Things

It would be ideal to store your pets' things in the utility room, if you have one, but make sure you store them away from any washing, laundry and your own things. Grab everything pet-related – leads, medicines, food, brushes – and then separate every category. Make sure you have a container for all the individual types of items, just as you would divide your own things. So keep their grooming things away from their food and safely store their medicines separately on a high shelf.

Cleaning Products

According to a study published in *Ideal Home*, the average household overspends on cleaning products by around £100 every year! That means there are either some very shiny houses or A LOT of spare cleaning products. Go through all your products and think about what you really need and what you actually use. Group the products you need to keep by room and return them to the shelf. If you have any spare new and unused products cluttering up your cupboard, donate them to charities tackling hygiene poverty or check if your local food bank is in need of household items.

Dolly Dash

Utility Checklist

**FUNCTIONAL AND FANTASTIC –
UTILIZE YOUR SPACE TO THE MAX!**

☐ **Chores not stores**
So many people turn their utility
space into a store room and fill it
to the brim with excessive
quantities of goods, from huge
bottles of fabric softener and
rolls of kitchen towel to cans of
Coke. If you give the space a
purpose (whether that's washing,
airing and ironing your clothes or
storing away all your outdoor
gear like waterproof jackets and
wellies), the space will work
harder and make your life easier
than all those stacks of multibuys.

☐ **Make a clean sweep and keep
the minimum you need**
As always, clear out the room
completely before you begin to
reimagine it. Only return the items
you really need.

☐ **Find ideas and inspiration**
Utility rooms can be tricky to
tackle as the practical functions
of the space leave us feeling
uninspired. If you're having a
mental block with the utility
room, head to Pinterest and
make a mood board of ideas that
could work in your space.

☐ **Seize every opportunity
for storage**
Utility spaces are often small,
but you can find storage
opportunities in the most
surprising spaces. Could you
hang a clothes airer from the
ceiling or add a rail to an alcove?
Could you add slimline, door-
mounted shelves to the inside of
a cupboard to hide away your
cleaning products? Assess your
space for storage solutions
before you begin.

☐ **The seven wonders of the
cleaning cupboard**
I'm a strong believer that you
don't need dozens of products to
keep your home clean and fresh.
My secret seven are: polish,
anti-bac spray, bathroom cleaner,
bleach, limescale remover, Fairy
liquid or Dawn, and Flash for
floors. That's it. Clear out any
duplicates and consider donating
excess products (see page 88).

Dining

Having a room you only eat in a few times a year seems so old-fashioned now. I think a separate dining room is definitely more important to the older generation. Many homes I organize want a dining space in the kitchen now because living and eating around the kitchen table is more important – unless you're in a really big house and do a lot of entertaining. People definitely need tables to eat from, obviously! But there is a big difference between how we live with formal dining tables and how we spend time as a family around a kitchen table. But either way, that time is precious.

I'll always remember the beautiful dark mahogany table in my dining room when I was growing up. It was extendible, so you could add an extra middle panel when we had people round at Christmas. We even had a little serving hatch from the kitchen into the dining room where you could pass the food through – that's definitely something you only see in older houses. (The house I live in now had a hatch when we moved in but we knocked through the entire wall to make an open-plan space.) There was also an elegant sideboard filled with all my mum's special china. My mum still has that sideboard – and the china – and we're moving it into the new annexe we are building for her.

I was always taught that quality things were made to last, and that's so true because that china is still here!

That sideboard and the china has been in our family forever and means so much to me. I'll always remember how everything was stored really neatly. All the fancy plates and old-fashioned cutlery... That sideboard was probably the neatest piece of storage my parents had in their entire house!

It was in total contrast to the dining table, which was where my dad worked and was covered in paperwork. Because of all the piles of work on that table, we rarely ate in the dining room, unless we had people round for a big family dinner. Most of the time we ate on our laps in front of the telly.

The dining room definitely wasn't somewhere we ate together regularly as a family and it definitely wasn't a room that was utilized to its maximum potential. I would love to go back to that house and rework the space now! It's time to work out if you could rework your dining space, too.

Clear Up, Dine In, Chill Out

Our house is a party house – we want to have our friends round all the time! We've even built a bar in the garden and it's fun and silly because I wanted it to be a space where you can relax. When the girls come round for dinner, all the spices come out and I cook up a little Sri Lankan feast!

Dining rooms are a luxury now, but eating at a table is good for us. It brings us together and can also encourage healthier eating habits. Whether it's a humble meal for one when you've taken time to set the table, or a big family dinner with all the trimmings, there's something special about a dining space.

Eating at a table creates time to share your day and talk through problems that might be cluttering your mind.

Once you have a clutter-free kitchen, it will be easier to cook for yourself, your family and your friends. But what's your dining space like? Answer the questions below and work out the best way to enjoy the room (and your food).

Does This Space Make Me Feel Happy?

» Is my dining space what I imagined it would be when I moved in?
» Has the table become a dumping ground for laundry waiting to be folded, homework and things I'm not sure where to put?
» Do I have a set of 'good' plates that are only ever used once a year?
» Is the space somewhere I can relax and enjoy a meal?
» Do we only eat here together on special occasions because there's too much clutter to use it all the time?
» Could I make the space work harder for the people who live here?
» Would it make more sense to repurpose the dining room as an office or playroom?

Let Go of Perfection 101

When you're organizing, your goal is for your house to be perfect for you – and that is very different from the sort of perfection you constantly see on social media. You need to let go of making everything Instagram-able. If the space works for you, it's organized and the aesthetic makes you happy, that should be enough!

With your dining area, you want the space to be pleasing to your eye and the opposite of stressful. There is a big difference between the sort of mess that can impact your mental health and a space being lived in. Instead of getting hung up on creating the 'perfect' space, when you go into each room I want you to do three simple things...

1. **Go in and sit in the space.**
2. **Look at the things you have.**
3. **Work out what you don't want to be there and get rid of it.**

Imagine you're trying to have a relaxed meal but the clothes airer is in the corner of the room. However tasty the food on your plate may be, all you're going to be able to concentrate on is the washing – which has been up for five days and you still haven't got round to folding it away. Any room that you sit in to relax needs to have the area around it completely clear to make the space less stressful. In fact, a clear view is what we are aiming to achieve in every room in your house, and it doesn't have to be perfect.

Don't Save
Your Best
for Best

Upgrade every day

We are all guilty of buying special things and then never using them, but why? At some point, you might invest in some really beautiful plates and glasses and while there are items you will save for very special occasions (because you're not going to drink your morning orange juice out of a champagne glass *every* day), what I want to encourage you to do is not save your best for best. Don't just keep these things to use once or twice a year. You worked really hard to buy these special things and have beautiful items in your home, so use them!

Maybe you need to upgrade your day-to-day essentials, then you could enjoy eating off your fancy plates all year round rather than just at Christmas! You could even buy some gorgeous plates for every day and then some really festive ones for the holiday season. In every aspect of life, I want you to enjoy your best items right now. So eat off your best plates, wear your beautiful dresses, go out in the fabulous shoes, use your posh face creams... You just don't know what's round the corner so you might as well enjoy what you have.

Make a meal of it

Stop for a moment and think about what you have in your crockery cupboard. Maybe there are beautiful plates that your granny passed on to you. If you never use them, they are just going to end up in a charity shop one day and that is such a waste. You don't have to get them out for breakfast, lunch and dinner every day, but even if you decide to use them every Sunday, you'll get so much pleasure from them. Each week you could use granny's plates for a special family meal. Just make the most of the beautiful things that you have. Life is so precious and we work so hard, as did the generations before us who worked hard to give us the life we have and the things we own. Those things should be used and enjoyed. They *shouldn't* be sat in a cabinet collecting dust.

Feel-good food

Think about your clothes – the feeling you get from dressing up and putting on something lovely gives so much happiness – and can make the people around you happier too! I think every day is enough of an occasion to put on a beautiful dress just to go to the shops.

Using or wearing something you love makes you feel good, so filter out the filler items. Remember how we tackled your wardrobe? I said you should only have clothes that you love and that make you feel good when you wear them. It's the same with your plates! You should open your plate cabinet and think, 'I love my plates, I can't wait to serve dinner on them and enjoy eating off them.' Great plates inspire me to cook better dinners too! There is so much psychology attached to organizing the things in your home. Having a load of mismatched, chipped plates is depressing and it can really affect your mood. Filling your home with quality items feels great and if you really love something, you'll be encouraged to look after it – which in turn will make it last longer.

When did you last Dolly Dash your cutlery drawer? (See page 100.) Are you keeping excessive numbers of knives, forks, and utensils in one drawer? What can be moved out? What can be recycled? Do you have a 'good' cutlery set that only comes out on special occasions? Why not use that every day? It's amazing how a small change can make a big difference to your day.

How To
Maximize Storage

1 Make some space
What if you don't have a dedicated dining room or your home is open-plan? Storing your dining items is no problem if you think cleverly. There are so many beautiful ways to display plates and glasses. Open shelving looks particularly lovely and even an open bookshelf will let you store your plates, cups, bowls and saucers. Floating shelves are brilliant, too. Keeping it looking kooky and not messy is important, so even if you're adding kitchen-type storage to your front room, add some plants and make it beautiful.

2 Raise the bar
Maybe your sideboard isn't how you imagined it. Maybe you want to transform it into a beautiful drinks cabinet with nothing but your special cocktail glasses. Or maybe you turn it into a little gin corner because you always pour a G&T after work on a Friday – or a Thursday, or a Wednesday... Each space in your house should be a special area that you can really enjoy yourself in and you don't have to worry about not having a dining room sideboard either – it really doesn't matter! Just add storage where you can and think outside the box.

3 Reset and repurpose
I organize dining spaces in the same way I approach any other room – clear, clean, reimagine. When you're ready to work on the latter, start by making sure you are using the space to its maximum potential, which means it's devoted to whatever it's used for the most.

If you only use the dining table to eat off once a year for Christmas dinner but the kids use it every day for their homework, make the space more kid-friendly. So many people no longer use their sideboards for plates, so if the kids are doing their homework in that room, turn your sideboard into an arts and crafts hub with all their school books and homework in there. It's far better to keep kids' stuff in one place instead of spread all over the house (which I know it is at the moment!) and have everything to hand. Always plan your space with whoever is using that area in mind and repurpose rooms for what is predominantly happening in there.

4 Clear your plates

When it comes to what you need and what you're storing, I think that if you are a household of four people, you really only need...

» **8 plates**
» **8 side plates**
» **8 bowls**
» **8 glasses**
» **8 forks, knives and spoons...**

Doubling the number of items according to the number of people in your house is more than enough! You have one piece that you're using and one in the dishwasher or stacked in the cupboard. I see so many clients that easily have triple the amount for the people in that house. The goal is to minimize your sets because the more plates you have, the more you will have to wash up. People can't help taking out fresh things until their cupboards are empty – because if there are cups to be taken, they will take them! Keeping an edited count of items is cost-effective and environmentally friendly because you're not wasting water by constantly running the dishwasher.

5 Reduce clutter, restore calm

Try to avoid filling your cupboards with stuff you don't need. In every room, the more you have, the more you have to do – whether that's washing up plates, dusting books or tidying toys. If you're constantly washing up, ask yourself why. I think back to the one-bedroom flats I have organized where the owners buy things as if they have a four-bedroom house to store them in! We give ourselves the extra work. If you find yourself never getting on top of things, constantly scrambling to catch up and never having time to complete tasks, who is responsible? We all have so much going on in our lives but the more stuff we add in makes it harder to keep on top of things. Reduce the number of items in your house and you'll find it easier to stay in control.

I want the advice in this chapter to leave you with a clearer space, storage solutions that work hard for you, and perhaps even a special feature that makes you happy every time you look at it (G&T anyone?). All these changes should add up to a calmer, more relaxing space. So when you do use the area for dining it will feel cozy, comfortable and inviting, leaving you free to concentrate on good food and good company.

Candles

To keep your beautiful dinner and scented candles burning brightly, wipe round the tops, trim the wicks so they don't splutter out black smoke and give everything a good dust.

Dinnerware

If you don't keep a close eye on dinnerware, you'll soon find you have enough to feed an army rather than four people... Have a dash for dishes, one for glasses and another for cutlery. When you dash your dishes, look out for any plates or bowls with cracks or chips. The same goes for glasses – you could also take the chance to polish them up. The cutlery drawer dash will probably involve removing junk that doesn't belong in the drawer (see page 74), but make sure all your spoons, knives and forks are divided correctly. Remember whenever you dash your dinnerware, think about how much you're storing and how many people live in your house (see page 99). Only keep what you really need.

Mugs

Mugs seem to multiply when left unchecked. Again, sift out any that have cracks or chips. Don't store more than you need and bear in mind that a matching set will make your cupboards feel neater.

Dolly Dash

Dining Checklist

CREATE THE PERFECT PLACE TO EAT OR TRANSFORM AN UNDERUSED SPACE INTO A MULTI-TASKING TRIUMPH

☐ **Enjoy your food**
If you're surrounded by stuff (a full clothes dryer, toys, homework...), it will always be trickier to turn off, tune into you family and focus on your food. Once you've cleared the table (and the room) of clutter, you'll finally be able to relax and enjoy your meal.

☐ **Dine in style every day**
If you have beautiful plates or gorgeous glassware, don't just bring them out for special occasions. If you use and savour them every day, they'll bring you so much more joy then they will collecting dust in the cupboard!

☐ **Step up to the plates**
Now is the time to clear up and clear out your plates, bowls, glasses and cutlery. If you double the number of each item in line with the number of people in your household you'll have more than enough dinnerware – and less washing up! Donate items that are still in good condition and dispose of anything with chips or cracks.

☐ **Dine and redesign**
If you have a dining room but find you only use it for dining a handful of times each year, reconsider the space so it works for the people in your house all year round. Would it be the perfect spot for a playroom or homework station? Do you need a home office space? Could you turn the sideboard into a bar so you can display your beautiful collection of cocktail glasses? Reimagine and redesign the space so you can have your cake (and perhaps a G&T) and eat it too.

☐ **Good enough to eat**
While a lot of people post beautiful plates of food (and images of their beautiful homes) on social media, please remember that your dining space doesn't have to be Instagram-perfect. As long as it's clear, clean and inviting, your meal will always be served at the best table.

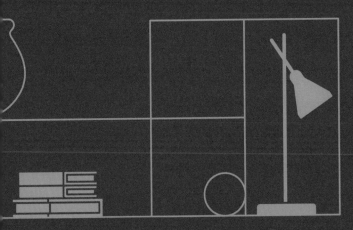

Living

This should be the ultimate room to relax in. A space where the whole family can congregate and hang out together is so valuable for your relationships. It's very important you keep your living room clutter-free, to encourage that mood of chilled-out togetherness...

I don't have many memories of my living room when I was growing up, mainly because my parents were always working, so we didn't do much relaxing together. They certainly didn't do enough relaxing. We had a formal front room for guests but the back living room, which led onto the garden, was the main living space. It was pretty basic. There was a cream carpet, which was really grubby because the dog was always running in from outside, and the TV was an old square box with five channels. (I remember when Channel 5 launched with the Spice Girls – it was amazing!)

This room certainly wasn't somewhere we spent time together as a family. It wasn't a beautiful calm space you'd want to relax in and we definitely didn't sit and watch box sets or binge on Netflix – it was the *Six O'Clock News* then *Coronation Street*, *EastEnders* or *Casualty*, followed by the *Nine O'Clock News*. My dad absolutely loved to watch cricket and football (he supported Tottenham Hotspur) so I'd watch it with him. But apart from those rare moments, it wasn't a hang-out room in the same way we use our living rooms today.

In my living room now, we'll all sit down and watch football or a film together. It's a family space.

My home today is so different and reminds me of the way my neighbour's house was when I was growing up. They had a beautiful living room with a Bang & Olufsen TV, two yellow Laura Ashley sofas and an interior designer had visited to plan the space perfectly. I spent more time there than in my own front room growing up! We only used our front room if guests came round. It had one strange oil painting, two sofas and a beautiful piano, which I used to play. I was a very good girl growing up and played the flute, saxophone and sang in church! Although I stopped being quite so well-behaved when I went to secondary school...

The goal here is to transform your living area into an easy-going, organized and beautifully aesthetic space that frees you up to watch your favourite box set, enjoy family time, or even read a book!

Make a Laid-back Living Space

Our way of living has become far more laid-back and we like to create rooms that are comfortable and chilled and that let us be together as a family – rather than devoting valuable space to formal sitting rooms we only use for visitors.

When it comes to tackling the organization of your living space, sit on your sofa – right now – and as well as those fundamental questions (see page 16) ask yourself the questions on page 107 and answer truthfully.

When you come and sit down on the sofa at the end of the day you want to be able to really relax in a calm room. What you don't want is to have to sit awkwardly amongst chaos with the stress of an untidy clothes horse blocking your view.

To achieve that Zen-like feeling, you need to curate the items in your eyeline, edit the number of things you keep in the space, and review how you organize the things you do need to store there. (All

I have in my living room is a sofa, TV and a console for books and the digital TV box.)

Living rooms normally have a sideboard, cabinet, console or bookshelves, and I've found they are generally more straightforward spaces to organize, especially compared to bedrooms full of clothes and kitchens full of equipment, but they can always be improved.

A room's structure often fails when random items creep in.

How are you organizing the stuff in your living room and is it really relevant to the space? Have you got lots of photos in your sideboard? Do you need to keep them in there? When did you last go through what you actually store in your sideboard? Work through the space and get rid of anything random as you go.

Always make sure your bookshelves only have books on them rather than stacks of paperwork or office files. I've seen bookshelves that hold medicines and nail varnishes, so gather up random items and put them in the right place.

Many of us are moving towards open-plan living and this brings its own organizational challenges. Are you maximizing the storage options? Open shelving is incredibly versatile. Maybe you could add a shelf to put books or ornaments on. This will make the room feel lighter and let any important items be displayed beautifully. You might decide to put your drinks on a shelf and turn it into a mini bar area – but if you do, make sure it's aesthetically pleasing so you can look at it with happiness.

Does This Space Make Me Feel Happy?

» Is my living room what I imagined it would be when I moved in?
» What can I see?
» Does the view make me feel relaxed or stressed?
» What can be improved in my eyeline?
» Can the bookshelf be neater?
» Can the side table be less messy?
» Do the kids' toys need to be hidden away?
» What can I change so the space is tidy and looks neat?
» Am I storing items in the space that don't belong here?
» Do I need more storage or can I repurpose the storage I already have?

Change Your View, Change Your Mood

A room with a view

Through my job, I've come across dozens of homes where you can't even walk inside the front room because it's so messy. There are so many people who have to move piles of paperwork just so they can sit on their sofa to watch TV. Sometimes they can't actually watch TV because the mess has become so bad it's unmanageable. I've even seen people bring out a little foldaway chair and sit on that instead of their sofa. How can that scenario be relaxing at the end of a busy day?

It's essential you make sure the view from your sofa is calming. If it's not, this is how you change it. To create a calm space, the room needs to be as empty as possible. You really only need your TV, sofa and a few ornaments or books. I'll explain how to arrange your bookshelves shortly (see page 112) but you need to keep things tidy. This is a room where you go to unwind as a family, so you don't want to be constantly looking at pockets of stress.

See things in a new light

Are your surfaces covered with stuff that shouldn't even be in your living space? Are there toys all over the floor? Is there enough storage or do you just need to update it? Do you need to create hidden storage rather than use open storage? Maybe you have a unit full of kids' toys that are overflowing from their baskets... can you change the baskets for something with lids, or rearrange the toys so you can't see them over the top of the baskets? Perhaps the containers need to match your front room and not look like kids' storage?

Switch it up

A quick fix to make your room look fresh is to upgrade your storage baskets. If you have an Ikea Kallax unit for kids' toys, I'll bet the containers are grubby and worn out, because your children will be constantly delving into them. If that unit is in your front room, think about how, if you switched out those drab containers for some chic baskets, it could actually look really pretty (and definitely not like a big piece of kids' toy storage). Let's face it, Kallax units are incredibly handy and affordable but they can also be unattractive, so any way we can add personality and make them match a room should be embraced. Once you've decided on the best storage solution for your space, don't overfill the containers. Now it's switched up, the new view should be beautiful, organized and calm.

Sitting pretty

You also want to make sure that you have invested in what you're actually sitting on. Your sofa is like your bed – it should be comfortable and supportive. Those cushions need to be fluffed. Every time I look at my sofa, I want to sit down on it because it's so inviting and I know that when I do finally sit on it, I'm not going to get up.

Also, how does the room smell? Scent can play a huge part in making a space feel calm. Think about the moment you open your living room door – what is the instant feeling you get from the living room and what does it do to your mood? If it's not a sigh of contentment, what can you do to change it up?

Think about creating little pockets of happiness around your room. Can you make a display of everlasting flowers and candles? You need to have things in your home that will make the space pretty and make you smile every time you look round. Think about what you can add to your living room that will give you pleasure – and then bring that into the space.

It should never take more than a day to catch up with chores for your entire house – but if you're thinking, I can't even get through one room in a day, there is a problem! You have too much stuff so you need to get rid of things. The less stuff you have, the easier it will be to keep on top of things.

Heirlooms 101

Avoiding the nostalgia trap can be tricky. Throughout your home it's vital that you don't let the emotions attached to material things overwhelm the importance of that item.

Everything in your eyeline should bring you happiness and be aesthetically pleasing. Maybe your late grandmother left you a vase that's not to your taste, but you feel too emotionally attached to get rid of it. First, think about whether it could go in another place in your house. If you can't move it, consider what you can add to it to make it more you? If it's an old vase, could a bunch of neon pink everlasting flowers make that vase look cooler or more modern?

How can you change things by updating them? What can you do to those pieces of furniture or ornaments that need a modern twist to stop them becoming a negative in your space? How can you rearrange, upcycle or reinvent them so they become something fresh and attractive to look at? You'll be amazed at how simple it can be to turn unloved heirlooms into items you enjoy looking at and will treasure for years to come.

Create Space for Multigenerational Living

Multigenerational living is on the rise, bringing several generations together to share one space. I left home when I was 19 and never looked back! But when I discovered how ill my mum was, I brought her into my home to live with us. It adds a whole new dynamic to our relationship.

But that means I really understand how you can create a calm home, even with three generations under one roof. The living room is probably the trickiest space to negotiate if different generations are together and open plan living is particularly tough.

Together apart

It's very important to divide the relaxing spaces for each generation. We got to the point where our living arrangements felt claustrophobic. Mum would want to watch something on TV but we wouldn't want to watch what she wanted to... and vice versa. It was awkward! We decided to convert the conservatory into my mum's sitting room, so she had her own private space, otherwise we were constantly on top of each other!

Can you create separate living spaces too? If you are all trying to do things in the same place it can cause tension and stress. If you can give each generation their own area it will give you all back the headspace that allows you to relax in the way you want. When you live with lots of people it's even more important to make time to unwind as personal time and personal space become rare.

How to Arrange Books and Records

1 Choose structure over style
The biggest collections of items we might have to keep in our living rooms are likely to be books or music, both of which can make beautiful displays. And for your books, you might think that starts with colour-coded shelves but it absolutely does not! If you're a bookworm, arranging your books by colour is the most confusing way to store them. Think back to your wardrobe. We arranged your clothes by type, so all your shirts were hung together, your blouses, your skirts... We only sub-divided those types of item into colour if you had loads of something. Once your shirts were together you could divide them into white shirts, denim shirts and brights, but if your whole wardrobe is divided by colour it's impossible to see what you have clearly.

Organizing your bookshelves by colour does look cute but you will never find what you're looking for! You can divide all your cookbooks by colour once that genre is all together, but don't organize cookbooks, spy novels, gardening and travel together, just because they're all blue. When you try to find Jamie Oliver's cookbook you will have to go to the blue shelf (if you can remember what colour each book actually is) and dig it out. Colour organization slows down the whole process of searching whereas the point of good organization is to give you back time. If you really don't care what books are on the bookshelf then fine, arrange in colour, but I don't know anyone who says, 'I'm going to sit down and flick through my green books,' whereas plenty of people will take time to bring out their interior design titles or fancy cozying up with a romantic novel.

If you're the sort of person who keeps lots of books, go through your collection and only keep those that spark real emotion. Those are the ones you'll pick up and think, 'I loved this book! I want to read it again!' Whereas there are plenty of others that are completely meaningless so it will be easy to give them away.

2 Gift your books

Certified bookworms and reluctant readers alike will have books that they know other people will benefit from reading or get enjoyment out of. I think it's lovely to pass books on and gift them to friends. It's a very nostalgic thing to do, especially today when we read so much digitally. I just gifted someone an old Sri Lankan cookbook that was battered and curry-stained – it made me emotional handing it over! As well as the cooking stains it has memories and meaning and the recipient knew what that book meant to me, while I knew how much she would treasure it.

Once you've gone through your books and decided what to edit out, can you think of someone to pass special titles on to, or can you make a gifting box outside your house for people to help themselves? Or pass them on to charity or community care services where you know they will be enjoyed. (Remember, anything you donate should be clean and in good condition. And it's always worth calling ahead first to check your items can be accepted.) Lots of items in your house hold a resale value and can – and should – be sold, but I believe you should pass books on to your family and friends over selling them, every time.

3 Ditch your discs

If you have DVDs lurking around your house, get rid of them straight away (local recycling centres don't currently accept them so donate responsibly). They are so old hat and a streaming service will save you so much space. While vinyl can be beautifully displayed, you can never make DVDs cool. Maybe you have boxes or cupboards full of them? Perhaps you have them stuffed in your TV cabinet? They take up significant and useful space! Once you've got rid of them, you could use that space to file paperwork or store a sewing box instead of a DVD you watched once and will never watch again.

CDs can go too. We used to buy thousands of CDs because it was the only way to listen to music but now even the older generations realize that streaming music is so much easier (and sounds better!) than filling your house with not-so-compact discs. You could keep a handful of CDs of really nostalgic songs that truly mean something to you (for me it would be TLC's *CrazySexyCool*), but you do not need to keep 400 of them. With every collection of things in your home, go through them and limit yourself to, perhaps, 10 items to hold onto as memories but you absolutely don't need to hold onto everything.

4 Play and display

Vinyl, on the other hand, will live forever! It might be bulky but it will always look modern stored in open bookshelves. There are lots of ways to organize your records: by genre, alphabetically by band/musician name, or alphabetically by album title. Again, pick the system that makes sense to you.

Is there a way you can create an amazing music area in your living room with decks and a record player? Perhaps with a neon light above the space? Maybe you could move some of the books from your bookshelves into your bedroom and then fill the space with vinyl. Obviously it depends how much you have and where you can keep a bookcase, but storing records in your house looks eternally cool, especially with a turntable incorporated into the display. But however you decide to store them, make sure it looks neat and aesthetically pleasing rather than a collection of random stacks, so you're creating an attractive feature.

We all need to take time to slow down and unwind – it's key to our mental and physical wellbeing. Once your vision of your living space is clear (and the view from the sofa inviting!), you'll all have a place where you can really relax and put your feet up. And you'll always be able to find the remote.

A TALE OF CHAOS TO CALM

Reorganize and thrive

'When I first got in contact with Dilly, my living room was unrecognizable. I have a small arts and crafts business and the living room had turned into a stock room – it was never meant to end up that way but it did. I couldn't even see the floor, which was completely covered by my supplies, and the space was unusable. I just didn't know how to sort it out and started sitting on a small sofa in our kitchen-diner to watch TV instead. I closed the living room door and let no one go in there. I couldn't face what I had let it become. It just became too overwhelming to tackle and I knew I needed help.

Dilly swooped in and helped me regain control of the space. She walked in, she looked, she evaluated and within minutes she was sorting. Dilly collated bags and bags of supplies, arranged them in containers and labelled each one. We then moved all the supplies to my spare room, where we created a functional, organized storage space. I don't know why I hadn't thought of it before? It was unused space! The thing with Dilly is how she deals with YOU as a person. She doesn't ask how or why the room got like that or make you feel embarrassed about the way the space looks. I don't know how she saw the end goal to create a new vision for my living room, but she did and she made that change happen.

I am beyond grateful I found Dilly. My business has thrived since she reorganized my space because I can now see my supplies clearly and can sell things online easily. Thank goodness she came before we entered the 7-week long Coronavirus lockdown measures or I just wouldn't have been able to maximize my sales. Dilly really is unbelievably talented at what she does. Everything makes sense now and my living room is an incredible space again that my husband and I can enjoy.'

Books

Go around your house and gather all the books that have wound up in other rooms and take them back to your bookshelves, then group them into genres. Always arrange your shelves with the heaviest books at the bottom working up to the lightest at the top. Group your travel books together, your cookbooks together, your gardening books together. If you do want to organize by colour, only organize by colour within each genre. So, you could organize your cookbooks by colour, but don't mix things up outside of genre, otherwise you will spend all year looking for the one book that you actually want to read.

Magazines

Gather up all the magazines from around the house. Ask yourself why you are holding on to each one. Are they something that you really treasure and read on a rainy day or are you keeping them for the sake of it? Recycle them or consider asking if your local health centre or community project would like them. (Again, always call ahead to check your donations are wanted and can be accepted.)

If you collect a particular magazine, arrange any issues you want to keep by date. Group them from oldest to newest by month and by year, and then divide them again by genre and title. For example, keep all the fashion titles together and all the issues of *Elle* together, all the issues of *Porter* together and so on. I have kept all the copies of *Vogue* from the year that my daughter Nelly was born and they are waiting to be framed – I want to get them all up on the wall as a memento of her first year.

Dolly Dash

Living Checklist

CREATE A RELAXING SPACE FOR THE PEOPLE – AND THE THINGS – YOU LOVE

☐ **A clear view**
You will never be able to fully focus on family time or that new Netflix drama if piles of ironing, untidy stacks of books or abandoned shoes are in your eyeline. If you keep the stuff you store in here to the bare minimum and switch up your storage so you can hide everything else away, you'll be able to sit back and relax in a beautifully organized space.

☐ **Remove random items**
It's all too easy for sideboards, bookshelves, consoles and coffee tables to become swamped by completely random items – newspapers, medicines, pens, bottles of nail varnish... Sort through rubbish to throw away, items to recycle, and items to return to their rightful place. Then think about whether you are using your storage effectively.

☐ **Chilled-out touches**
Whether it's a gorgeous scented candle or a special heirloom you've updated with a beautiful bunch of everlasting flowers, fill the room with little pockets of happiness.

☐ **Make yourselves comfortable**
If you're living in a multi-generational household and have room, create separate living areas so you can all unwind in your own personal space. It's also very important to invest in what you're sitting on. So find a comfy, supportive sofa, fluff those cushions and hit 'play next episode'...

☐ **Calm and collected**
When we curate and organize our collections properly, from books and music to gallery walls, we create attractive displays from the things we love that help us feel more relaxed and 'at home' in our living spaces.

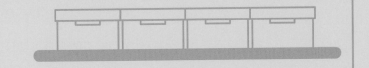

Entrance

Your hall or entrance space is the first thing you see when you open your front door. It's the place where you can shed your outer persona and begin to be the real you as you relax at home after a day at work. But more often than not, it's a magnet for clutter that sets the tone for the rest of the house.

After I came back from getting married in Bali, I visited my mum's new house in Somerset for the first time. I just remember seeing so much stuff in the porch. She had been living there for a while but because she always came to visit me, I'd not seen how she was living, which was in total chaos. I realize now that by always visiting me, she was hiding the mess – and the extent of her mental illness. She was surrounded by stacks of unopened letters and piles of unopened parcels that spread down the hall. As I went further in, I found stockpiles of vitamins, boxes and boxes of face creams, a carrier bag full of iTunes gift cards (all with the codes scratched off) and more carrier bags of bundled up receipts. The stuff totalled thousands of pounds.

My mum had been a victim of fraud and given away around £50,000 to scammers. She was told that by giving away all those iTunes cards, the scammers would fix her computer. Likewise, she'd send £4,000 to China or Spain via MoneyGram and never see what she'd been promised. When I spoke to the police, they said there was nothing they could do. I was devastated. That hall was a physical representation of the state of Mum's mental health and the rest of her house followed suit.

People can get themselves into all sorts of messy situations and the state I found my mum in was heartbreaking. Her house had gone beyond the clutter I remembered from my childhood home to a whole new level of 'Oh my God' despair. It was just the most horrendous way to live. My husband Charley and I decided to move Mum to our home, where we are building her an annexe. The reason I work so hard is to give my family, and especially Mum, a lovely life. Clearing her house is how my career in organization began. That was the moment I realized that there are SO many people who have to move piles of papers just to watch TV or who can't even make it through their front door because of the stacks of books in the hallway.

Think about your hall as the beginning of the journey, the first step into your organized home.

The goal of this chapter is to make sure your house puts its best foot forward, so when you first walk into your hallway you feel safe, relaxed and happy to be home.

Make Your First Impression Count

The hall is not only the first space in your home that you walk into, it's also the space that can really influence other people's perceptions of you. Think about the first thing people notice when they walk through your front door. If it's a porch full of piled-up coats and stacks of shoes, is this the first impression you want to give to your visitors? Is it a reflection of you? Is the hallway a representation of what the rest of your home is like? If you want it to be a calm, tidy space you have to properly utilize it. It's time to make your entrance an entrance.

People's hallways are often clutter-magnets. So think about the space and the questions at the bottom of page 123. Then work out how you could improve the space. Look around, consider the clutter and identify your personal flashpoints. Here are the top seven clutter culprits....

1. **Dozens of coats draped over the end of the stairs.**
2. **Scattered piles of shoes.**
3. **Stacks of unopened mail.**
4. **Countless keys – you're not sure what they open but you can never find your front door key...**
5. **Bags to take to the charity shop (that** have been sitting there for six months).
6. **Bags of online shopping returns.**
7. **Your kids' football boots (even though they grew out of them last term).**

Once you've identified your flashpoints, finding storage solutions that work for you should be straightforward. Could you add coat hooks or shelving? Could you add a shoe basket to a nook instead of stuffing things behind the door? Reimagine and restructure the space.

Next think about what you can do to change the aesthetic of your hall. My childhood home's hall was very small and all the mail just got piled up on the windowsill by the bottom of the stairs. There was always stuff on that windowsill but it is so important to keep windowsills clear. Windowsills need to be pretty! Think of them as a frame to whatever view you have – you want your frame to be beautiful so it enhances the view. Can you arrange some plants or flowers on the windowsill? Maybe add a candle and a photo? Anything but piles of mail!

Whether your hallway is spacious or small, you have to work hard to keep the clutter out. When you plan your new storage it's really important to do thorough research on what you're buying. Make sure it will work in the space and hide the clutter. You may dream about a console table in your hall but in reality is one small drawer really going to hide all your stuff? Bulky furniture can also make a space feel claustrophobic.

Aim for a light and airy feel and whatever you can do to get that feeling, do it.

Take everything out of the space and picture your entrance as you wanted it to look when you moved in. How can you get it to where you want it to be? What changes do you need to make? As you answer these questions, you might see how you could move things around to free up a space you could fit 20 pairs of shoes into!

We want to reduce entrance clutter and introduce the best storage solutions to keep it under control, so you can feel calm whenever you enter or leave the house... and always find your keys.

Does This Space Make Me Feel Happy?

- » Is the space what I imagined it would be when I moved in?
- » How do I want people to feel when they walk through the front door?
- » How is the space organized and am I using the space effectively?
- » How could I minimize clutter?
- » Are there lots of coats but not enough coat hooks?
- » Are there piles of shoes but no racks?
- » Is there hidden storage or is it all open?
- » If it's open, what can I see?
- » Could I make it neater?

Use Your Under-stairs Space

Perhaps you're reading this book now and the intensity of your situation – or that of a friend or family member – is becoming clear. If your house is messy, this book will help you get back on track. But you might be beyond that stage and have moved to a point where you can't get in through your front door anymore.

This is when you need medical and professional help, along with the support of your friends and family. Look back at your childhood. It might be tough but perhaps you can recognize traits or habits that have made you more than just 'a bit untidy'. Organization is a truly life-changing process. I want you to realize the importance of correcting any underlying issues. Once you have addressed them, you will be able to create the headspace you need to begin to conquer clutter.

For details of organizations that can provide support, see pages 180–181.

Right now, do you have an under-stairs cupboard that's so full not even Harry Potter could live there? What is in there? I bet you have an accumulation of pet paraphernalia, sports stuff, cleaning products, an old pram, some random DIY tools... and a cuddly toy! The problem with shoving lots of different types of things into one area is that none of it is properly organized, so when it comes to locating that tennis racket, you'll have no idea how to find it.

Makeover magic

Can you reinvent the under-stairs space? You could book a company to come and help you make a really effective storage area. But do you just need to add coat hooks or shoe shelves? Maybe you need a coat rack or perhaps you can take the coats out of the hall completely. If you're lacking space, you need to make sure you're making what you do have work hard. Would it be more efficient if you turned your under-stairs cupboard into a pantry? I've done that on a couple of occasions for clients. Effective storage all goes back to working out how to make the most of the space.

Overhaul Your Shoe Storage

Shoes are always going to be a problem, especially if you have a large family with kids. There is always going to be mess by the front door because you need to keep shoes close by... But is there a way you can organize them?

Divide and conquer

You might be able to find a storage bench that sits neatly in your hallway that allows all the shoes to be tucked away. Or you could search for a slimline, wall-mounted cabinet. But always try and make sure everyone has a place for their own shoes. Divide whatever storage you choose – shelves, baskets or containers – so everyone has a designated space. You could put each person's shoes into a different basket and maybe the baskets are hidden away in your under-stairs cupboard. Each family member should know they have to chuck their shoes in their own basket when they come home from school or work. This will stop you scrambling round to find your shoes amongst a melée of trainers, slippers and football boots. When I introduced the Trail of Destruction, remember that feeling of chaos in a home can be exhausting. Finding a matching pair of school shoes in the morning is a pretty stressful situation but if you can just divide the shoes – and avoid the mess – you won't have that issue anymore.

How to Keep Mail and Keys Under Control

1 You've got mail... organize it!
I'm as guilty as everyone else of ignoring the post. I hate opening mail. I'm not good with money and I never have been, so the mail fills me with dread because most of the time, it's another bill. Mail is a negative for a lot of people because not many of us want to open our bills and give away our money, do we? It's not often you get a letter that says, 'You've won £5,000!' Bills can be daunting and that's why a lot of people struggle to deal with them. But you can do it.

2 Create a sorting system
The most important thing you can do to stop yourself getting overwhelmed by mail is opening it and actioning it as soon as you can. It's great to have a little organizer by your front door for post and as soon as it gets full, you know you need to go through it and file it away. But only give yourself a small organizer or make sure you only allocate one small drawer for your letters. What can happen is anything you keep your mail in can start to overflow, so keep the space small and neat. As soon as you take everything out, action it, deal with it, then file it or recycle it. I have a system that my husband deals with the mail and then I file it. Could you introduce a similar system in your house? Once everyone knows what their role is and takes responsibility for their task, sorting the bills will feel straightforward rather than scary!

3 Go paperless
Look at what's coming through your door and contact each company sending you paper correspondence. It takes five minutes to call or write an email to switch to paper-free. Go paperless for your bank statements too and go online with everything you can. (See pages 136–137 for more advice on going paperless.)

4 Click to unsubscribe

Unsubscribe from as much junk mail as possible. You could even put a sign on your letterbox saying you don't accept unsolicited post. This will reduce the amount of stuff coming into your house because, let's face it, most of it will go straight into the recycling without ever being opened. It takes a few minutes to get taken off a mailing list, but the amount of time you spend taking junk mail to the recycling bin can get frustrating. Not only is junk mail a waste of paper, it's a waste of a company's time and money, and it's adding to your stress. Unsubscribe to reduce the clutter coming through the letterbox and your mail will immediately be more organized.

5 Safety is key to success

It's always cute to have a little pot for your keys by the front door, but from a safety point of view, you should find somewhere out of sight and out of reach to keep your keys. You might think you're hiding them somewhere clever but most of the time it's very obvious where people store their keys. If you don't want to keep your keys by the front door for fear of being burgled, consider finding a spot away from the letterbox and door that isn't somewhere people will think to look. But it also needs to be somewhere you will remember! Perhaps you will choose a pot inside a kitchen cupboard – you can even buy little key safes. Wherever and however you store your keys, always keep them together. And always return them to the same spot.

6 Customize your keys

Label each key so nobody will ever end up confused about which set is which. Colour coding your keys works really well, too. Likewise, make sure everyone has their own set of keys that are identifiable to you (and them), but not to anyone else who might be snooping around.

It's important to make the most of our entrances and hallways. Even though we don't spend much time there at all, if you can step into a clear, organized and welcoming space you'll feel happy to be home – and happy inside.

The Car

Grab a black plastic bag and collect all the empty water bottles, the sweet wrappers, the random kids' toys, shoes, tissues, parking entry tickets, shopping lists and receipts... Remember the 'Three Rs' – get rid of the Rubbish, Recycle what you can, then Return everything that has escaped from its proper place back to where it belongs. Check the boot. It should be clear, apart from your reusable bags for life, ready for when you go shopping. It's also really handy to add a container into your boot to store your kids' football boots or the muddy boots you only wear for walking the dog. Back in the car, make sure you empty your glove box and wipe out down the sides of the seats. Vacuum the seats and foot mats, if you can. You could even add a lovely, naturally scented air freshener too.

Dolly Dash

Entrance Checklist

SET THE TONE FOR YOUR HOME WITH AN ORGANIZED ENTRANCE

☐ **Make a good impression**
Your hallway should be a reflection of you and your home. Pinpoint your clutter flashpoints then find the best storage solutions to tidy things away. Clear the windowsill and add some finishing touches (a beautiful picture, candle, mirror or rug) to create a welcoming space for you and your visitors.

☐ **That's the size of it**
Be realistic about the size of your entrance. You might love the idea of a console, cabinet or bench, but if they don't provide the practical storage you need or overwhelm the space, you'll end up with an entrance that feels cramped and confined rather than airy and inviting. Consider storage solutions carefully and pick ones suitable for your space.

☐ **What lives under your stairs?**
Often the under-stairs cupboard is home to a muddle of coats, brooms and sports equipment. If you give the space purpose (coat closet, cleaning cupboard or even a pantry), you'll transform it from cluttered cave to effective storage area.

☐ **Don't let shoes takeover**
Use shelves, baskets or containers to divide up shoes and keep them under control.

☐ **Unsubscribe from disorganized mail**
If your entrance looks more like a sorting office, go paperless whenever possible. It's better for the environment and better for you. Have a designated place for post and a system to action it.

☐ **You've got the keys...**
and the secret to keeping them organized is: give everyone their own set; label them clearly; always keep them in the same (safe) place.

A dedicated office is the dream but even if you only have a corner of your kitchen, the goal is still to create a space that is clear of clutter – and unwashed dishes. If you try to work surrounded by unorganized paperwork it's harder to focus and concentrate. If you work from a crowded desk, that will affect the way you work too. Likewise, if your laptop is balancing on a load of paperwork, you'll be distracted. Maintaining an organized space and a healthy work-life balance is vital to your productivity, creativity and wellbeing.

I've always been surrounded by work in my home. When I was growing up my parents were accountants and although my dad had an office in Southall, he brought his work home and turned the dining table into his desk. There was paperwork everywhere, and it spilled into every single room, including my parents' bedroom. And today, for many people the dining or kitchen table often still doubles as the home office desk.

But I've seen first-hand that how you work in your home can really affect your family life and your health. My parents lived together and worked together and I think that was hugely detrimental to their relationship and triggered both their illnesses. While he was alive, my dad (unintentionally) worked my mum into the ground. While my mum would never admit how hard it was (for her generation, that's just how marriage worked), it really was her downfall. She worked too hard and she couldn't cope, so it made her ill. Overworking made my dad really ill too.

In my experience, working with your partner – in your home – has a negative impact on your relationship. There is never any escape, you're never not talking about work. It's hard enough to manage all the normal relationship/family/house/admin worries without bringing in working woes too! I know some make it work, but for my parents' mental health, it was the worst thing they ever did and it's something I never want to repeat.

Yet working from home has become the new normal, if only for a portion of your week. Some people need absolute silence, structure, a proper desk and a closed door to get things done. A lot of people work from outside spaces because there are so many interruptions at home – although there is bustle and noise, they are less distracted in a café than in their own house.

Obviously you might prefer – or need – to be around people rather than working solo, but if the only reason you're heading out is because there are too many disturbances at home, we need to ask: why is your house so stressful? What can we do to change that? Maybe the kitchen is too chaotic or your study too messy to get any work done. How can you bring calm to that space? Work is stressful enough without having to factor in 'where' you can work just because you haven't got round to sorting it out.

We need to make sure you have a space that works hard for you.

And even if you're not performing a job in your house there will still be council tax, gas bills, bank statements and car insurance documents to deal with, which will all benefit from having office-like organization. Let's get to work!

Write the 'Job Spec' for Your Space

No matter where your WFH (working from home) space is, we simply can't be as productive when we have chaos around us! My office space is actually my kitchen island, so if I have any work to do at home I am in the hub of the house. I'm not hidden away but I have to make sure the surfaces around me are completely clear or I can't concentrate.

However you work and whatever your job is, it's crucial your working from home space is clear and organized.

What is your current WFH space like? When you come to define your ideal home office, think about your current set-up as well as the type of environment you need to have a really productive 'day at the office'. Think about your space – and the requirements of your job – and then answer the questions at the bottom of page 135.

If your current WFH space isn't working, do you need to find a different place in your home that will allow you to be productive and enjoy your work? Maybe you have somewhere in mind already. Is there a spare room overflowing with clutter that would make a great home office if you transformed the space? Perhaps you could carve out a desk area in the space under the stairs, in a corner of your living room or even on the landing? Sometimes you need to be creative to create space.

So, how do we achieve an organized WFH space? What do you need to do to that room or area to make it a functional working office? Our actual jobs determine what we need to work. Say you're a writer, maybe you just need a desk and a laptop. Or if you're a maker, you might need reference books, tools and space to move. What about bookshelves for all those reference books to be organized properly? If you need to tackle a lot of admin, do you need a filing cabinet for all your office paperwork? Think about the storage solutions your line of work requires and make sure you have some sort of filing system in place.

It's also essential to think about how you can make the space pleasurable to be in. How can you make it somewhere beautiful so that you can focus (and even enjoy!) getting on with the task at hand? Could you position your desk near a window so you have natural light – and maybe even a view of nature? Think about adding a plant, photograph, or an amazing art print that inspires you. The ideal is to create an area that not only you can use, but your children and whoever else is in your home, can all utilize too. But the ultimate goal is to give you a space with as little distraction and as much inspiration as possible.

Does This Space Make Me Feel Inspired And Energized?

» Is the space clear of clutter, or am I constantly surrounded by magazines, homework and dirty dishes?
» Which items and storage solutions do I need to work efficiently?
» Where is my WFH space? Is it a separate room or a corner of the kitchen table?
» Is the space what I imagined it would be when I moved in?
» Do I need to move my home office to be more productive?
» Do I need complete silence to work?
» Do I need to be tucked away so no-one disturbs me?
» Am I productive in communal areas surrounded by noise?
» Where am I happiest working and where can I get the job done?

Digitize
Your
Documents

Out with the old...

There will always be some rogue paperwork in your home that needs to be filed but how long do you keep bank statements for? Do you really need paperwork from last decade? (I know you have some!) I don't use paper bank statements anymore as everything lives online. The only documents I keep are insurance policies and I only keep this year's and the previous one. That's all you need! Last year serves as a reference of what the costs were, then as soon as this year is up, I get rid of the previous year.

... in with the new

If you can digitize your paperwork and file it online it will – obviously – reduce the amount of clutter you have to deal with in your home. Set aside a morning and go through all your bills and invoices.

Would you like the receipt?

Make sure you're not keeping receipts for things you're never going to take back. Unless it's an item of great value, you don't need your receipts. Neither do you need food receipts after seven days. Clear out your purse and recycle them if you can, but remember not all receipts are recyclable.

To stop yourself drowning in receipts in the first place, try to get an e-receipt instead of a hard copy. It's better for you, and better for the environment. And if you're asked whether you want one at the till, never accept one unless you really need to. Whenever I go food shopping, I always say no to the receipt. Nine times out of ten you're not going to take anything back and even if you do find a mouldy strawberry in the punnet, it's unlikely you'll take it back to ask for a refund. Driving all the way back to the supermarket to change a punnet of strawberries will cost more than the £3 we paid, so we just tend to shove it in the food waste and move on.

Satisfaction guaranteed

Make sure you're not keeping receipts for the big-ticket items you bought last decade. But if you have made a recent purchase, keep your receipts organized. Create a receipts folder then divide it into electricals, furniture, jewellery... However you arrange the file, just make sure that if you do need something, you can find it easily as and when you need to. This should make seeking a repair or replacement as simple and stress-free as possible – and you won't have to ransack the house for the relevant paperwork before you start. As soon as the item is out of warranty, get rid of the receipt! It's useless, unless you are planning to sell it on and you want to keep the receipt as reference. But even then, most people don't want them.

As well as going paperless for your bills, you should digitize your kids' artwork too. Lots of people struggle with the emotional attachment to our children's scribbles and can't throw those pictures away, but keeping every single painting will take up so much space in your home.

If you have a particular favourite drawing or painting that brings you a lot of happiness, you could save the original and frame it. Gather together the rest, take a photo of each one and upload them to create a neat photo book of their work.

I know you'll want to keep some things, but it's important to regularly revisit the things we save. The way you feel about something today is not the way you will feel about it in six months' time. You might come back to your memory box and certain craft projects or collages spark up real emotion and you'll continue to keep them, but you really don't need to save every washing up bottle rocket. You won't miss them! Your kids won't miss them either because they don't remember much of their early years. Talk to them about organization and then ask them, 'Is it OK if I get rid of this?' You'll discover they are often far less emotionally attached to things than we are as adults.

Don't Let Work Affect Your Relationships

Set and respect boundaries

It's so important to set boundaries and create your own space when you're working from home. If you live with someone who is also WFH it's vital. You both need to have separate areas where you can retreat and know not to disturb each other. So, be honest with each other. Who really needs the space more? Who needs to stay at home for their work? It's tricky, but you both need to create some sort of system so you don't overtake each other's areas. If one of you is a blogger, for example, and creates lots of video content at home that could interrupt the other's Zoom calls. Check in with each other at the start of the day so you can be as considerate as possible.

Go 'out of office'

Good organization is more than just arranging stuff, it's scheduling in ways to give each other mental space too. Perhaps you take it in turns – you work in the morning, they work in the afternoon. Or offer to go out so your partner can stay in and take calls. Maybe one of you can make your office a third space, like a café, library or co-working office. Often I've found people who work from home don't actually work from home, as leaving the house to work motivates them, makes them more productive and is better for their relationship. When you start to argue over working at home (when there isn't enough space or the kids are running around), remember your relationship is more important than a conference call. Don't give yourself the stress of trying to balance WFH and being in a busy household and take your work out of the house if you can.

Teamwork

Creating an area to work isn't just about you and your needs. You have to consider whoever else is in the house and adapt very quickly, whether that's changing a spare bedroom into an office or moving a printer onto a worktop in the kitchen. It's not just us and it's not just our space. We are hot-desking with our own family and need to manage the space – and manage ourselves – carefully so it doesn't have a negative impact on anyone.

Working in an office, or anywhere outside the house, allows you to be selfish. You leave, go somewhere else and concentrate on yourself and the job in hand. At home we have to think about flatmates, partners, children (and whoever else we share our house with) when we simply try and take a call. It's hard finding that balance. My husband is the worst for interrupting my work, especially when I'm doing an Instagram Live. He wanders in, makes breakfast really loudly and leaves a mess all over the worktops, all while I'm discussing how to declutter your kitchen! He'll be on the phone to the plumber, 'Yeah mate, just come round at 3pm,' while I'll be hissing, 'What are you doing?' At least my followers can laugh about it.

There will always be a battle over whose job is more important. That's why it's so important to bring division, structure and organization to your office space.

Nowadays most of us just need a laptop, but even if you only need a laptop, what surrounds us is very distracting. If you are in an office that has stacks of books and paperwork, or stuff that is non-work-related like piles of clothes or washing up, this will have a negative impact on the way you work. Your mind needs to stay focused. Everything that surrounds you needs to be organized and the space should be as clear as possible to help you work better.

How to Create the Ultimate Office Space

1 Location, location, location
When it's time to create a WFH space, think of every available place you could work, whether that's a spare room or a corner of the living room. So many of us are creating cabins at the bottom of our gardens and if you can do that, great! But you could also think about creating a workspace in the area under the stairs, where you can turn your back to everyone and concentrate. Alternatively, you could add a couple of shelves to a wall next to a side table and make a little nook for you and your laptop.

If you're going to transform an existing space, think about where you want your desk. Is it in the best position? Are you working in natural light? Do you have a background that will look professional for video meetings? Experiment until you've found the best place.

2 Reset the space
When you've found the right spot, the first thing you need to do (as always) is to clear the space (and your desk) completely and create a fresh space to work with. Again, by clearing the space you can see what you need to do to add structure. Give everything a good clean, then slowly start to add things back. Only return what you really need. That might be a laptop and a lamp or a little filing tray. Then think about how you could make your workspace more inviting, so you want to be there – perhaps you could add a candle, a plant or a vase.

3 File it away

When it comes to your paperwork, gather it all together in one big box then you need to sit and sort it out until it's all divided into sections. By creating a filing system you will bring structure into your office. All your stuff should be filed appropriately by category (finance, utilities, work, your kid's school and so on), and to make it even more effective you could colour code each category. You could add in a file for each member of your family – including the cat! However you want to arrange them, just make sure that everything is organized. You could add a filing cabinet, so you can put the relevant documents into sections, or you could add floating shelves so those files can be arranged there for easy access.

4 Run a tight ship

Make sure everything has a place so next time you go to your desk you only need to turn on your laptop to start work. You might decide to add a bookshelf so all the reference books that are scattered around the house can be neatly arranged, along with your files. Find a space for your papers, your shredder and your contracts – rather than one huge, chaotic melting pot. An organized space will help you work so much more efficiently and easily. So... when can you start?

Taking the time to find and organize a home office space is always going to be a smart career move. You'll feel more in control and less stressed, and your space will also promote better focus, concentration, productivity, creativity – it could even improve your sleep. It's true what they say: tidy desk, tidy mind.

Your Paperwork

Paperwork piles up so quickly, but you can clear your desk in 15 minutes. The best way to Dolly Dash your desk is to collate all your paperwork, which could be scattered all over the house in multiple piles, then put it in one file or box. You can come back to the box another day, when you have time and space to sort out each individual item because it's easier to work with one pile than it is with many... But right now we are focused on giving you a space that you can work from and getting your desk back to being clear, not cluttered.

Office Supplies

Even though you can never find a pen when you need one, more often than not stationery ends up all over the house. So gather together all the pens, pencils, notebooks and sticky tape that were originally spread around the house and put them in a craft box, divided into their groups. You might have 15 rolls of tape, 14 pens, a pencil for every day of the week and enough notepaper to write a novel, but because they are kept together in a container – and you can see exactly what you have – you know that you don't need to buy any more. And you'll always know where to find a pen!

Dolly Dash

Office Checklist

ESCAPE NINE-TO-FIVE CLUTTER AND CLEAR UP YOUR WORKSPACE

☐ **Find the right space**
Whether you like to work in the hub of the house or tucked away in a silent corner, find or create a designated workspace to increase your productivity.

☐ **Pick the right tools for the job**
What do you need to help your work day run smoothly? Filing cabinets, open shelving, a bookcase, a peg board? Write a list of requirements for your space and set to work.

☐ **Don't make extra (paper) work**
Digitize your documents whenever you can, don't keep receipts unless you need to and clear out expired warranties. Clearly organize essential paperwork you need to keep – file by category and consider having a folder for everyone in your household. You'll avoid papers stacking up and won't have to turn the house upside down to find that vital warranty.

☐ **Work together**
Sharing your office space doesn't need to be a deal-breaker – remember your relationships are more important than emails and video meetings. To keep things running smoothly, discuss your to-do lists, set and respect boundaries for each others' workspaces and consider whether heading 'out of office' for an afternoon would be more productive.

☐ **Get down to business**
Once you've found the right location and storage solutions, reset the space. Clean it out, clean it up and keep it clear and organized. Add a couple of inviting aesthetic touches like a plant, print or candle. You'll have an inspiring space that's free of distraction and that everyone in your home can utilize. Job done.

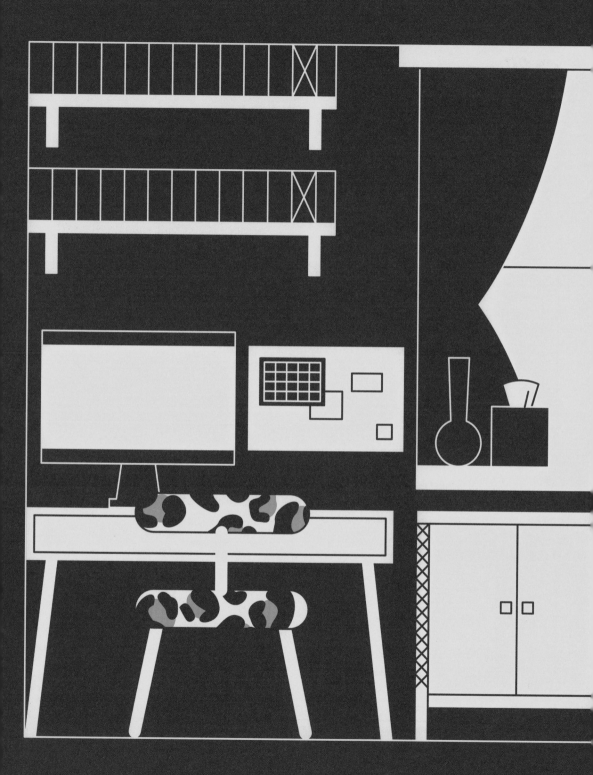

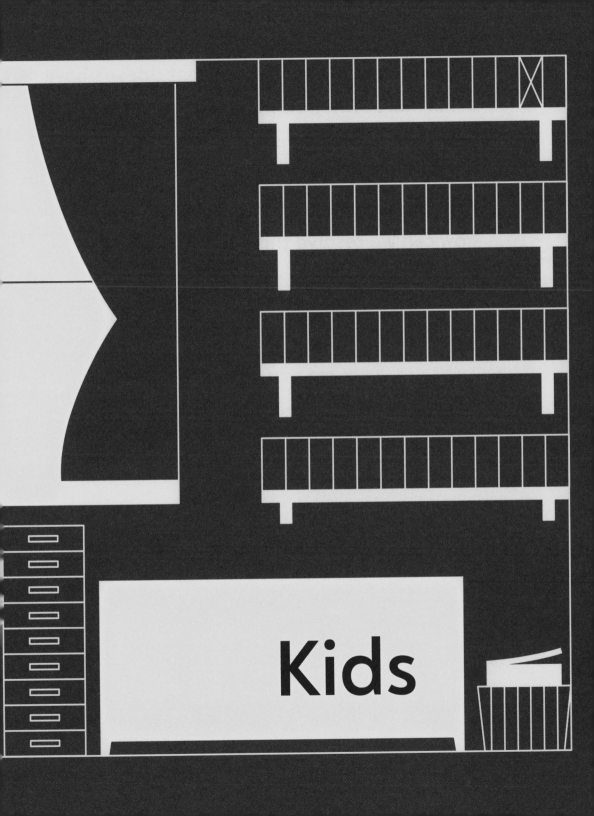

Kids

There is a room in my house that doesn't have a minimal aesthetic and I admit I really struggle with it. My bugbear is my daughter's room. It's full to bursting with toys! Our homes are drowning in toys and mine is no different, so how can we resolve this?

When I was little I was always trying to tidy. Whenever I could, I would tidy. I tidied to try and make sense of the mess in my adoptive parents' house – because there was so much physical clutter around me.

Before I came to England, I spent the first three years of my life in an orphanage in Sri Lanka. I was raised by nuns in a convent that relied on donations so there wasn't much of anything and there certainly weren't many toys. One of the earliest pictures I have is of me with a group of children and we are all playing with the same solitary toy. Fast-forward to my home growing up and there weren't many toys there either. I probably had a few teddies but I certainly did not have the same volume of toys Nelly, my six-year-old daughter, does.

Throughout my childhood, my mum taught me about the importance of buying quality. My parents didn't buy me loads of things all the time but, as I got older, when my parents did treat me it was usually a big splurge. My dad would take me on a shopping trip to Topshop once a year to get a new season's wardrobe. I was one of the first people I knew to get a mobile phone and my parents let me have their brand new SEAT Ibiza when I turned 17. Everything I had was of high value and even now my mum is still passionate about buying quality. My husband Charley is the same; he would rather wait and buy something more expensive and truly useful.

It's quality over quantity, whether that's with clothes, furniture or toys. And we need to instil that mindset in our children too.

But this generation of children are harder to please, they constantly want more because they're being exposed to more through advertising and peer pressure. Now children will get dozens of presents at Christmas. It's ridiculous! As parents it's natural that we want to give things to them. It's not like our parents didn't want to give us presents but there just weren't as many toys or opportunities for them. There was perhaps one shelf of kids' stuff in the supermarket. Now there are aisles and aisles of toys. In the past, many toys were wooden and built to last, but compare that to today. Millions of tonnes of plastic is generated every year, just for children's toys.

Having to tidy up toys is a temporary stage in our lives and I'm constantly reminding myself that my daughter is only little. She's not going to be into toys for long so I have to embrace that and let her enjoy them while she's small. We don't want to stop our children being stimulated or halt their creative side by not letting them play – the goal is fewer toys of better quality that really get used.

Go Back to School

From the moment our children go to nursery, they have a coat peg, a name tag and a tray and they understand that everything goes back in its proper place. Our children know where to find their bag. At the end of the day the Lego blocks go in the Lego box, the soft toys go in the soft toy box, the pencils go in the pencil pot... Organization starts on day one of nursery, everything has a place, and that structure continues throughout their whole time at school. So why isn't it the same when they get home? Raise your hand and ask the questions at the bottom of page 149.

If, like in most homes, there is no structure or routine when it comes to tidying the kids' rooms, why is that? Why don't we teach our children the same way they learn at school? They are taught about organization and accept it and follow those rules throughout their school-life, so we need to encourage the same methods of organization at home as well. It doesn't have to be as regimented as school but everything needs its own place.

If you've ever complained that your children are disorganized, it's not true. It's just that they haven't been given any structure to follow. Children like structure, they like routine and they need it! They need to follow guidelines – says the woman who still lets her six-year-old daughter sleep in her bed! Hands up. I admit I'm the worst when it comes to disciplining my own daughter because it's really hard...

But if you can try to create a system with structure and divide the toys as much as you can, not only does it make tidying up faster and easier, it will also help your children become considerate partners or housemates in the future. If you're not teaching organization now, someday they are going to be living with someone and be the person who doesn't know where anything is and has no clue where things should be put away.

It's so important to teach organization from a young age so your children know there is a place for their pants and their pyjamas and their school shirts. If your children just open their drawers and are scrambling to find a matching pair of socks, this is a task you can help them with.

Try to create structure for your children wherever possible. Keep all the things of one type together so they are easily accessed.

When I organize a kitchen, I always ask if the kids are at an age where they can help out. Whether it's storing the cornflakes in a space where they can reach them or putting all the cutlery together so they can lay the table, little changes that enable kids to help out can be big confidence boosters. If you can get them involved and help them take responsibility for their toys too, it allows them to help you, gain independence and learn organizational skills that will stay with them until they are grown up. There really is a lot we can learn from school.

Does This Space Make The Kids – And Me – Feel Happy?

» Is the room what I imagined it would be?
» Are there so many toys in here that I can't see the floor?
» Do I regularly step on plastic (and rather painful!) toys?
» Is there enough storage for all the toys, books, games and art supplies?
» Are the storage solutions clearly structured and easy for my kid(s) to access?
» Do they understand how to put their things away?
» Do we tidy together?
» Do we have a tidy-up routine?

Why Are We Attached to Toys?

Guilt and giving in

It's pretty safe to say that our grandparents' generation stayed at home more than we do, so they could give their children more attention. Now, when most of us work, I definitely think we feel guilty as working mothers or fathers. So, when the weekend rolls around and your children ask for stuff, you buy it for them! There are also the bribes we are guilty of offering our children: 'If you're quiet when I'm in my meeting, I'll take you to the shop later.' Or, 'If you play in your room while I make this phone call, I'll buy you that toy.'

But rather than using any toy as an incentive or reward or to ease our feelings of guilt, we need to get better at making sure the presents we buy our children are actually something they will play with and enjoy for a long time. Encourage your children to have toys that are better quality, rather than giving in to buying a magazine every week from the supermarket. There's always an enticing – but rubbish – toy on the front, which they play with for a day and then chuck to the bottom of the toy box. Instead of buying the magazines, why don't you offer the chance of something more expensive – like a figurine they love – at the end of the month? You'll save money in the long run, get something more valuable at the end and have less toys cluttering up your home.

An important lesson

Teach your children about the value of what you buy along with the importance of longevity. Children's toys are expensive but by buying quality, you'll end up with treasured items that will hold their value – in every sense. Having fewer, better quality toys will also help your kids learn to value their belongs and encourage them to take care of them. Plus, unless they have really bashed them about by the time they've moved onto another type of toy, the resale value of quality toys is likely to be good. Try to keep them in good condition and they will sell.

As with everything we organize, I want you to think about quality over quantity. Really think about what you are buying your children before you shell out. Consider the resale value and in turn, teach your kids the value of buying quality from a young age.

Don't look at the price tag

The real reason we struggle to get rid of toys is because we know the cost of them. If you look at a room full of toys, what you see is thousands of pounds. We know we splashed out £100 on that toy at Christmas which, two months later, isn't being played with. But we are reluctant to get rid of it because we know the monetary value. We also know we will never get the full cost back. So it's us who worry about getting rid of things because of our financial attachment.

Let it go...

We have an emotional attachment too. Toys evoke special memories of our children, especially on their birthday. Children really aren't as emotionally attached to toys as we think they are. If you offer a child something new, they will jump at the chance. If you say, 'Today we're going to get rid of five toys but I'm going to buy you one amazing toy to replace them,' they're really not bothered about clearing out old things. As long as they think they are getting something new, they'll do the clear-out. It's when you say, 'I'm going to take all your toys away,' they will understandably struggle.

It's hugely important that we acknowledge that we can often be guilty of buying toys to make up for lost time. That's the main reason our homes are full of so many toys! Toys are our bargaining tool, a 'sorry for not being there' or making amends. It's easily done but make sure material possessions are not your only bargaining tool.

Think of experiences rather than possessions. Instead of saying, 'I'm going to buy you a toy because you've been really good,' decide to do an activity together where you can have fun, learn something or simply be together. If you're using bargaining tools, swap those tools from physical possessions to time well-spent. All our children really want is for us to sit on the floor and play with them. They are actually not that needy. Kids are simple creatures and they don't ask for much.

If we can offer them experiences, they are going to be much happier than having actual things that they will get bored of quickly, and they will remember those experiences for a lifetime.

The bank of Mum and Dad

It's not children who struggle to get rid of toys or bring them into the house. It's us! We are the only people in control of buying toys. When we are trying to tidy and think, 'There are so many toys,' we are the ones to blame. Sorting toys is hard and I struggle with it as much as anyone else. I am a mother of a child who loves rubbish plastic toys so I completely empathize with every parent. But there is a way to keep them under control...

Keep the toys kids love

Although Nelly has lots of toys, I make sure that she plays with everything she has. She has an L.O.L. Doll obsession – it's been going on for years and she still isn't bored of them. I don't mind the money I spend on the dolls because she is always playing with them. Nelly also has three dolls houses. That's excessive! But again, she sits there and plays with them every single day. It's fine to have lots of toys but make sure they are played with. The minute she stops interacting with something, it's gone. The problem with toys mainly comes when there are stacks of things that haven't been touched for a year that your kids are no longer attached to. Those are the toys that will leave your house untidy and will make you frustrated and stressed. Keep on top of their interests and go through the toys every six months – or more often if you can.

It's far better that they're playing with physical toys than glued to a screen, although I've got nothing against tablets... anyone who says that their children don't play on them is lying! We all shove our children in front of a screen when it suits us and Nelly learns so much from YouTube it's ridiculous! Our kids need to be tech savvy and we all rely on screens for work. There are so many secondary schools where every pupil has a tablet and many lessons take place on a computer. As they grow, you'll see your children go through the general toy stage then move onto gadgets. They will all want Nintendo Switches, PlayStations, iPads and Kindles one day soon, so this messy toy stage will come to an end. Believe me, when they get even older, all they will want is a really good mobile phone and that's all they will care about!

Whenever I go into a playroom that needs organizing I don't think, 'Why have you got so many toys?!' I get it. I know exactly why the toys are there. But don't let your feelings deter you from reducing the volume by removing things that aren't getting played with or being treasured. If you regularly edit the toys and clear out unloved items whenever you get the chance, you can let the kids have fun without feeling frustrated.

Teach Your Kids Decluttering 101

When we take time to educate our children – or people of any age – and explain why we are organizing things, they will understand. Keeping your home clutter-free should be the responsibility of everyone in your house, so when it comes to doing a clear-out of toys, talk to your children and prepare them.

I think it's lovely to donate as a family. Explain how you want your children to choose five things to donate and reassure them you're going to choose five dresses and your partner is choosing five things to give away too. Go round the house together and choose things, point out what is not being played with anymore. Then incentivize the donation by saying you will all treat yourselves to one new thing – or perhaps go out for a family meal – once you've made the donation. I promise they will be OK with this!

Don't just say, 'We are having a clear-out and getting rid of some of your toys…' Take time and give your kids a reason.

Explain where your donations are going. Perhaps there is a charity shop nearby or a local community project you are passionate about. It's important we clear clutter and organize in an educational way, so talk to your kids about the cause your donations will be contributing to. You may be helping a hospital, hospice, animal shelter, church, emergency service, local sports team or school; perhaps you'll be helping to combat homelessness or further medical research or human rights causes; or maybe you'll support a children's, crisis or mental health charity.

Describe to your children how your donations could help others – perhaps even family and friends. Through the simple act of decluttering, you'll have taught them empathy, kindness and compassion, as well as a really important lesson on the value of decluttering and how it's something you should do together as a family.

How to Organize Toys

1 Reimagine the space
Look at your entire home and think about where the toys could live. Have you got a spare bedroom that your children could keep their toys in? While a playroom is a luxury, organization boils down to working out what is most important and what will help make life easier in your house. Perhaps you have three kids so it's more important to turn that spare room into a playroom instead of an office because the kids' toys are all over the place and causing you stress. It's all down to how big your house is and how you need to organize your home.

2 Think outside the (toy) box
Children's storage doesn't have to be big, bulky and made of plastic. You can find really attractive storage solutions for all the kids' toys. If you have the luxury of a playroom you might not be so hung up on the aesthetic, but even if something stores toys, it doesn't have to be a toy storage unit! I've seen some beautiful chests of drawers and sideboards that toys are organized in. When the drawers are shut or the cupboard doors are closed, you wouldn't even know there were children in the house!

3 Find practically perfect storage solutions
Your toy storage solution will come down to budget, how you want to organize your house and the style of your home. If your front room is overrun with toys and you have a mid-century modern aesthetic, think about a sideboard that looks like it belongs in the room. If you need your storage to be practical and versatile, think about buying something basic you can adapt. Ikea's Kallax units, for example, are so useful at dividing toys up into different sections, and could be used to store school work and stationery when your kids are a little older. Your storage solution should also be easy for the kids to use – this will help them learn to tidy their toys away and give them a sense of achievement and responsibility.

4 Use the power of invisibility
The most important thing is that you are buying storage that allows things to be hidden from sight. This is doubly important if the toys need to live in the living room. Whatever you choose is down to you, but if your personal living space is being taken over by children's stuff, you need to change things up.

5 Toy storage

When it comes down to individual toy storage, break down the toys into type. So you've got containers for Lego, Playmobil, Paw Patrol, Disney characters, Sylvanian Families, L.O.L. Dolls, Barbies, remote-controlled electrical toys and so on. If you can break it down further it will be even easier to find that one toy your kids are desperate for – and quicker to tidy everything up. That means dividing the Lego into different colours for bricks and another section for characters and accessories... Can you find a small storage tin for Barbie shoes and clothes, so they don't get lost in the bigger Barbie container? Make sure you have an arts and crafts area and that paints and pens are separate from the soft toys. The more you can group things – in every area of your home – the more organized your space will be and the calmer you will feel.

Remember, the goal isn't just to have a tidier house, it's to enhance your children's play time, encourage their creativity and teach them to care for the things they value. When you stop toys taking over the house, you clear the way to make more time – and space – for fun.

School Things

School things end up scattered around the whole house throughout the week so take 15 minutes on a Friday to gather them all up and store them in their proper allocated area so they can always find their books and files easily without your help – and without fuss.

Bookshelves

Get everything grouped into genre – picture books, nature, annuals, fiction. They should never take more than 15 minutes to arrange neatly and it's a really quick win.

Toys

Get your kids involved when you Dolly Dash toys and take the opportunity to edit out unloved items – they will be much more inclined to get rid of toys than we are! Remember, they are not financially attached to their toys and the money that was spent on them. When I Dolly Dash the toy box, I always edit out goody bag toys and those plastic free gifts from the front of magazines.

Dolly Dash

Kids Checklist

TACKLE THE TOYS AND HAVE SOME (ORGANIZED) FUN

☐ **Do your homework**
Letters, numbers and organization! Though we may not realize it, we start learning how to be organized as soon as we reach school. From coat pegs and paper trays to lunch boxes and pencil pots, there's a place for everything and it's all tidied away at the end of the day. Create the same structure for your kids in their rooms. Teach them where to put their toys, books and clothes. Tidy along with them and give them an A+ for their efforts.

☐ **Swap toys for time**
Often we buy toys because we feel guilty for not being around, or we use them as an incentive or a reward for good behaviour. But try offering time together instead. Whether it's a family outing, a baking session or simply joining in with play time, if you share, play or create together your kids will be happy (and there will be fewer toys to tidy).

☐ **Fewer toys, more fun**
Keep a close eye on your purchases and make sure every toy you bring into the house will be treasured and add value to play time. Monitor their interests too. When your kids completely stop playing with a toy, edit it out to leave them with a toy box full of the things they truly love. Once again, quality not quantity is the name of the game.

☐ **Super storage**
As long as you can hide toys out of sight and your kids can easily and safely access them, you can think outside the box when it comes to storage. Consider a sideboard, chest of drawers or an ottoman. Group toys by type as much as possible, so finding and tidying them away will be child's play.

☐ **Give together**
Decluttering and donating together as a family is a great way to boost your children's confidence and nurture empathy as they learn how to organize and share.

Spare
Spaces

This chapter comes last in the book because we're going to talk about the 'spare' spaces we don't encounter every day during the Trail of Destruction – spare rooms, lofts and garages. They're places you might venture into at the weekend, once a month or even once a year. You open the door, shove something inside and quickly shut the door on the mess again. Although they are so often overlooked dumping grounds, these spaces could become some of the most valuable rooms in your house.

I think a lot of people probably have the misconception that I am super-, super-organized and on top of absolutely everything. While my home is very organized (everything has its place and there's a minimal amount of everything), my life can still be quite chaotic! Especially when it comes to personal admin: it can take me half an hour to join a Zoom call, I still keep a paper diary, and I can be terrible with names. But I'm good at going into chaotic situations and knowing how to change them.

Spare spaces are usually storage spaces, filled with all the things we never know where to put.

If you have the luxury of a spare room, I bet it is never actually spare because I know you've filled it with rubbish. When it comes to spare spaces, lots of people have a mental block. Often we never really know what's in the loft or the garage and only one person in the household is brave enough to enter – allowed to return only once they've found the suitcases. So, where are you going wrong with your spare spaces and what do you need to do to fix them? Do you need to repurpose the spare room, or do you need to sort out your storage solutions in the garage or loft?

Spare spaces are so valuable, especially if you are struggling with storage in the rest of your home. So often you think that you can't do anything with them, but visualize what these rooms would look like empty. What would it be like if everything was clearly labelled and everything had its own designated place?

We all have our own personal chaos, but the simple act of decluttering can make a huge difference by giving you a clear space – and a clear mind – to deal with it. The goal is to have beautifully organized spaces that you can use for whatever you wish, or well-organized storage areas that will create space in the rest of your home.

Transform Spare Spaces

Spare rooms, lofts and garages are spaces we don't go into very often but when we do, we often struggle to find things and waste hours searching for one item. Instead of just filling them with the items that don't have a proper home, start to think about how you can use your spare spaces to your advantage. Think about the questions on page 163.

Giving your spare room a purpose will allow you to create structure in the space so you can actually enjoy using it. Whether you decide you need a beautiful guest room so it's easy for family and friends to come to stay, or a comfortable snug to retreat to and relax in, if you give the room a clear function you can utilize the space to its full potential.

Great organization, utilizing storage solutions like shelving, clothes rails and containers, is vital in a loft or garage. So rather than arranging these rooms as big open spaces where you're not sure where anything is, you should be able to go in and know exactly where the photos are... You know where all the skiing stuff is... All the camping stuff... And the children's favourite toys you can't part with yet. So many people just store things in black plastic bags then throw them up in the loft, but the problem with this is that you never know what is inside them!

We need to create a system so that everything in your loft, garage or spare room has its own allocated space.

The key to creating an effective storage system in your loft or garage is, once again, to remove and go through every item, grouping everything by type. When you've edited the items and know what you want to return to the room, you need to make sure the items are protected from dust and dirt, easily accessible, and can be found instantly. Always use clear plastic tubs to divide your items, then label them so it's easy to find whatever you need: split up the soft toys from the train set; divide your clothes into seasons; keep your shoes separate from your bags. Grouping things into smaller sections makes things so much easier, so when you do want to get your summer dresses out of the loft you'll know exactly where they are and you won't have to wade through suitcases, bin bags and boxes to locate them.

Imagine what it will be like to head straight to one tub and find what you're looking for right there! If you can add a rail to your loft, do it. If you switch your wardrobe over with the seasons, it will make life so much easier. Use a clear clothes protector to cover the whole rail so you can see what you're looking for and still have easy access. I am obsessed with coats so I have a rail in my loft of all my outerwear. They're not packed into tubs or shoved in black bags, I can just take them off the rail and swap them in for things I have downstairs. When you have a rail in your loft, it's a game-changer!

Whatever you decide, you need to make sure your spare spaces are utilized and organized properly – so they never become dumping grounds again.

Could My Spare Spaces Improve My Home Life?

» If you have a spare room: is it an unloved space full of random items?
» What do I have in excess?
» Could I turn the spare room into a playroom for all the kids' toys?
» Do I need an office because I work from home with lots of resources?
» Could the spare room be dedicated to books or vintage magazines and be turned into a cozy reading room?
» Could I dedicate the spare room to my hobbies and store all the arts and crafts materials or all the gym and yoga equipment in there?
» Is the loft and/or garage a well-ordered and well-organized space?
» Can I find things easily? Or do I have to fight through fairy lights, tools, toys, tennis rackets and old clothes?
» Could I add storage solutions to transform these spaces?

Blank Space and Structure

When you moved in, I bet you just shoved everything into cupboards. Although it never really worked and you wondered how it could be better, you never did anything about it. Until now. Nine times out of ten your rooms can all function – and look – better. But you can never complete that change until you empty the whole space and start again. Emptying the space allows you to see the room in a different light and will help you see how it could work better for you. This is why we must go through the clearing process, so we can envision the room as a fresh, new space. It's impossible to organize on top of things that are already there. When you're looking at a load of stuff it becomes stressful. You always need to make sure you are working from a blank space to change things up.

Clear the way

With any room I'm organizing, I always go in and clear it first. This is as important for spare rooms, lofts and garages as it is for kitchens and bathrooms. I work from the left to the right and clear every single surface. I've even been known to spread the entire contents of a (overly cluttered) garage over the drive. So move all the stuff to one side or get it out of the room entirely if you can.

Why do I recommend you do this too? Before you start, you need to give yourself a clear working space so you can physically see what you have and give yourself the headspace to plan a new vision for the room. A clearer space helps you work more effectively. Everyone works from a clear desk more effectively than they do from a cluttered desk. Everyone sleeps better in a clear room rather than a messy one...

Working with a blank canvas

Clearing the room is so important for large spaces like lofts and garages. With the entire contents of your loft, for example, spread out in another location, you can transform the empty space before you into an organized haven that will really work for you. Seeing that blank space is inspiring and allows you to reinvent the whole area. That is the true value of clearing the room first.

Don't forget to think about the furniture in a room too. Yes, we all have bits and pieces cluttering up our space but is the furniture the problem? Is the bed too big for the spare room? Is the chest of drawers taking over the space? Have you got any bulky furniture you're never going to use again and could resell or donate? Sometimes you might have *too much* storage but we can't see those problems until you've taken everything out.

Smart structure in big spaces

Once your room is empty, you can start on the transformation. Look at the empty space and decide how you can achieve the structure you want. Ask yourself: how can the space work harder for me? Let's think about how you might structure your loft space. You might decide to put your memory boxes to the back of the room because you don't need to access them often; then your overflow wardrobe goes in the middle where the ceiling is high enough for a rail; while the camping stuff goes near the hatch because it's bulky, so it will be easier to retrieve and return if you don't have to drag it past boxes of (breakable!) Christmas decorations.

However you decide to arrange your loft, garage or spare room, it has to be organized in a way that makes sense for you, with a structure that makes everything easily accessible.

How to Sort Sentimental Things

1 Don't be filled with indecision
Most of the items you store in 'spare' spaces are things you can't make decisions about. Sports equipment you're not sure where to put, folders you're not ready to get rid of, boxes you might need again one day... It's very important to keep revisiting those undecided items because the way we feel about something today is not the way we will feel about it tomorrow, in six months or a year's time. The same applies to items of sentimental value that we might be using our spare spaces to store.

2 Revisit and review
Our emotional attachment to things changes daily, weekly, monthly... If you review your sentimental items once every few months, you may find you're ready to part with something you previously wanted to hang on to. Perhaps you were keeping a bag of clothes you used to wear before your kids were born that you had some amazing times in. Now you might be ready to acknowledge that they don't suit your lifestyle or don't fit anymore. If you're never going to wear them again, it's time to let them go.

3 See things in their best light
It's a mistake to think that you can tackle going through personal memories in your loft or garage. The two tasks are very different. When you are sorting out your loft, you're organizing it to create space and structure – whereas going through decades of personal memories needs time. You definitely can't do that in a stuffy, dark space. Bring them into bright, clear, comfortable surroundings, so you can see things in their best light.

4 Save special memories
We often keep memory boxes in spare spaces. There will be so many things that the connection has faded from among items that still make your heart pound. The latter are the things you should keep because they are irreplaceable and as long as they are in a clearly organized, allocated space, you can continue to keep and treasure them.

5 Take time with your photographs
We talked about creating displays around ornaments with sentimental value in the Living chapter (see page 110), but things like photos can be harder to deal

with. If you have a box (or four) of old photos in your loft or garage, it's essential that you take them out of that space to go through them. Bring them downstairs and tackle them when you have a clear block of time, your favourite box set on in the background and a glass of wine to hand, perhaps with some family members around to help you identify relatives in older pictures.

6 Edit your images

I'm from a generation that has loads of printed photos but out of one roll of 48 frames, there are probably only 20 that are any good (this is probably true when it comes to the camera rolls on our phones too). The remainder will have redeye or be a double or have a blurry blob on them – your thumb, perhaps? By going through them all, you ensure that you keep the ones that are most valuable. This means you can reduce your collection right down so it takes up less space.

7 Mark the occasions

Buy a photo organizer before you start. Then as you go through the photos you want to keep, label them and organize them. Cornwall 2015, Christmas 1999. Spilt the photos up so when they go back in the loft they are organized and anyone else looking at them will understand where and when the memories came from.

8 Share special memories

Instead of having four cardboard boxes you've now just got one, and instead of all those boxes of 'OK' snaps, you have one box of really special pictures. Perhaps you could frame some or duplicate them for your family? In fact, getting your whole family round to be involved in the sorting session is a really enjoyable way to organize photos.

Sorting dark and dusty spare spaces, especially those housing emotional memories, can be daunting. But when you return these rooms to blank spaces, you shine light on the ways they can be repurposed to make your life better. When your spare spaces have a clear function and are clearly organized, when you actually know what's in there, they will be a weight off your shoulders – and possibly off the rafters too.

Coats

If you can, take your coats out of your wardrobe to give you enough space for your everyday clothes. Coats take up so much space so ask yourself, can you move them elsewhere? Perhaps they could go into a closet in your spare bedroom or on a rail (with a protector) in your loft. When you're ready to rehang them, make sure you group them by type – so all your trench coats are together, all your waterproof coats together, your heavy winter coats together – and then hang them from heavy to light, moving left to right. This is the most practical and aesthetically pleasing way to hang them.

Hangers

Something you can do very quickly to create a calm and clutter-free space is to swap over all your hangers to matching slimline velvet hangers. Remember my job is to help you CREATE more space and five slimline hangers take up as much room as one wooden hanger. The swap makes sense, right? It will take you 15 minutes to swap over an average-sized rail and will look so good – you will also be able to fit more clothes in your wardrobe. I do sometimes use the traditional wooden hangers but only for winter coats.

Donation Items

Today's Dolly Dash could be the day you action your charity piles. That bag of clothes or bric-a-brac that has been languishing at the bottom of the stairs or filling up the spare bedroom is going! Today is the day you will drive to the clothes bank, the charity shop or the hostel and responsibly and thoughtfully donate your good condition items (see page 182 for more advice).

Dolly Dash

Spare Spaces Checklist

TACKLE THE ATTIC, GET TO GRIPS WITH THE GARAGE AND MAKE THE MOST OF YOUR SPARE ROOM

☐ **Clear out the place and create thinking space**
It's often hard to feel inspired by our spare spaces. Clear everything out and look at the empty space with fresh eyes. You'll be surprised by how quickly you'll reimagine it.

☐ **Give 'spare' a sense of purpose**
If your spare room is underused or unloved, think about its potential and give it a purpose. What would make your home life easier? What would make it better? From a home office to a playroom and a reading nook to a beautiful guest room, make sure you're really utilizing – and enjoying – the space.

☐ **Garage groups**
Grouping is a key part of organization everywhere in the house, but it's particularly key in the garage where you're likely to store a wide range of different items – from the toolbox and DIY kit to bikes and unused furniture. Group items together by type to create a more effective, more efficient, space.

☐ **Structure spare spaces**
When you're ready to reset a space like a loft, think about and identify storage solutions that would make the space work harder for you: consider clothes rails, shelving and containers with lids. Then think about the flow of the layout. Keep items you use frequently at the front near the hatch (like suitcases), and those you need infrequent access to (like memory boxes) at the back.

☐ **Take care of your memories**
Organizing items like photographs and memory boxes are emotional tasks. Always: take these items out of the spare spaces they are stored in; create a relaxing environment to sort through them; edit them down and organize them clearly so you're left with a really special collection; consider asking family and friends to help.

Calm

A Clear Path

Remember the Trail of Destruction you encountered at the start of the book? Instead of chaos and stress, imagine if your day began with calmness and serenity... You wake up rested after a refreshing night's sleep because, at last, you've been able to sleep. As your eyes open, you see fresh flowers on your bedside table and the delicious aroma from last night's candle still lingers in the air. Snuggling back into those fresh sheets and fluffy pillows for a moment, you really don't want to leave your bed, but you mosey on into the bathroom – with no piles of paperwork or work debris blocking your path.

You grab your toothbrush and easily find your moisturizer. You open your wardrobe and get dressed in a matter of seconds. All your clothes are neatly arranged and you can find an outfit effortlessly. Now you only have pieces that make you feel amazing, you know your outfit will make you feel fantastic all day long.

You wander downstairs without having to worry about tripping over a random piece of Lego and make yourself breakfast. You could whizz up a smoothie or have your favourite cereal, but whatever you decide, it's simple because all your breakfast things are stored together. Then, instead of leaning against the worktop while you wolf down a slice of toast, you take a seat (no need to move anything to find a chair) and admire your clean surfaces now all the random mess has been removed.

In your car, the empty water bottles and crisps crunched into the carpet are gone. You put on your favourite music and drive calmly before literally skipping into your workplace. You feel amazing and ready to tackle anything the day throws at you because you are well-rested, all the items you came across felt special and considered and everything in your home was accessible. Life feels easier at last.

Instead of waking up and feeling like you have a million jobs to do, if you've followed my methods, your home is now in order. Now when you wake up your focus is on the day ahead. There's nothing hanging over you! Instead of having a to-do list that needs to be actioned, your home is already in shape. Not having to worry about all the tasks at home means you can focus on your job. You'll no longer have to spend hours at the weekend catching up with the washing and tidying because you're on top of things.

Every item in your home has its own place and your house has structure. You have less to do because you have less stuff.

> **By clearing out the things that don't truly matter to you, the things that aren't really needed, the things that were causing you stress, you can enjoy your home again.**

I can't stress enough that the less you have in your home, the less you need to do. Keeping your home organized means it's easy to tidy and when a chore does need to be actioned, it never takes long. You no longer have to cancel plans because you need to spend all your free time catching up with things around the house. At last, you can focus on planning fun things and fill your evenings and weekends with family and friends.

Realize Your Vision

As you've worked through this book, where has your vision of your home taken you? Does your house now look how you dreamed it would? Have you reached your goal yet? Now you've reached the end of the book, your home should be exactly how you imagined it would be when you first moved in and before clutter took control. If not, we need to go back through the book together and again, envision your dream for every room. This time, do not stop until you are where you need to be.

The chaos I grew up surrounded by means I still have a vision unrealized... and that is to buy my parents' old house and transform it into the beautiful family home I always knew it could be. I never got the chance to do that because my parents were in such a state, they had to leave their home. They never had the time or the finances to make that house work for our family. But if I could go back and buy that house I would do it in a heartbeat and turn it into the inviting, organized space I always wanted it to be.

Whenever I'm back in Shepperton, I drive down my old road and treasure the moments I spend just looking at the house. It holds so many positive and lovely memories, despite all the challenges. And I know that all the things that I couldn't change at the time, I could change now.

I desperately wanted to bring structure to my childhood home but never got the chance. I'll always be longing to go back and change things so if you can change something while you still have the opportunity, do it.

I'm giving you this information because you are in a position to change how you are living right now. Your chance is still within reach.

And although I can't go back to that house, I've bought structure to my own home now. As messy as my house gets – and of course it gets messy with my daughter, husband and mum living under one roof! – everything still has its own place. When I need to tidy, I know what the vision of that room should be and I don't stop until I make that vision a reality.

You're reading this book because you were unhappy with your home. Or perhaps you didn't know why your home was so unorganized. This is where I hope I, and this book, have helped you. Now you know how you can make your home work for you, you should absolutely go for it and make those changes. My home is far from where I want it to be right now but I am working on it. It's important to know that your home is always a work-in-progress. Nothing happens overnight. There are changes to be made but knowing how to tackle a space is the best way to start.

Create
Space

By the time this book is published my mum will be – finally – living in her own annexe, in the home we have been saving for years to build. When the building work on Mum's annexe started, the excitement level was off the scale. Charley, Nelly and I have never lived in this house together on our own, so the annexe is going to be life-changing. We couldn't have bought this house if it wasn't for my mum's financial help and although the change will be strange, it will be lovely to have all this space for just the three of us – plus the dog!

And it will be so valuable for Mum too. She will have her own space and her freedom. It's been lovely that over the years I've been able to pay her back for everything she has done for me. My chosen career has allowed me to help her go from a home that was chaotic and making her very ill, to a place where she can be happy and focus on looking after her mental health and wellbeing.

My career has helped my whole family and I'm so grateful for what I've been able to achieve through my job. I've seen the benefits of my organization methods first hand, through the improving mental health of my loved ones, so I know that everything I've written in this book and everything I discuss on Instagram can really change your homes and your lives. I want you to feel the same benefits, and even if you're not as unwell as my mum was, I want you to feel happier in your home – and maybe help your family too.

Looking through my career, every negative I encountered, which I thought was holding me back, has turned into a huge positive. My parents were too busy

to pick me up after school so I hung out in the local store until closing time and packed bags for the shoppers – learning vital organizational skills and starting my decluttering journey in the process. Working in a designer clothes shop taught me how to fold clothes properly. Managing a beauty salon taught me how to manage people and delegate to a team. Doing admin in private households was where I ended up organizing kitchens, wardrobes and offices...

Everything I've done since leaving school at 18 has been focused around organizing. All those jobs that I thought were just minor detours have turned into major experiences on the path to building a career I absolutely love. That career has afforded me the luxury of being able to create space for my family to thrive. That's the best result of all.

Resources

Look After Your Mental Health

Create a support network

Everything I've taught you means you should be well on your way to a clutter-free home. Or perhaps you're now ready to go back to the start of the book and get organizing. However, if at this point you've read this book and are still struggling – you know you want to make changes but still don't know how – you need to ask for help.

Please call in a professional. You might be at the point where starting to declutter is beyond you. You know everything you've read rings true and you know the advice I've given you is solid, but you can't achieve those goals alone. This is when you need to book a professional service to help you.

Maybe you need a cleaner or a housekeeper, or a babysitter who can look after your kids once a week while you focus on your house. Perhaps you need to pay someone to sort, iron and fold your laundry? Whatever you need to do, whoever you need to help you, call them. There are so many ways you can save your mental health rather than struggle through and try to do it all. We can't do it all! We need a support network. We need childcare and cleaners. It's no problem to call in a plumber or a builder when we need help with the mechanics of our homes. It needs to be the same when it comes to clearing away the clutter. (See page 192 for more details about the help and services Declutter Dollies can offer.)

It's OK to ask for help

I say this constantly throughout the book and online, but you should never be afraid to ask for help if you are struggling with your home or your mental health. I can help you to a certain degree, whether that's in person or through reading this book. This book is all about clearing your home for better mental health and getting rid of the clutter to clear your mind. But if you're still having trouble, you need to speak to your GP or healthcare provider. When there is an issue beyond your control, that goes beyond having a messy aesthetic, please call your doctor.

There are different levels of help you can get – from my organizational skills, through to professional mental health advice. There are also charities that are ready to help you. Both MIND, the mental health charity, and Bipolar UK, a charity dedicated to sufferers, families and carers affected by bipolar disorder, are close to my heart and are here for you.

bipolaruk.org
mind.org.uk

Donate Responsibly

When you are decluttering your home, please donate items responsibly. If you want to donate to a charity shop, wait until the shop is open and don't leave anything outside to get rained on and damaged, leaving it impossible to sell and the charity with the cost of getting rid of it. It's always worth calling ahead to check that the shop is able to accept the type of items you wish to donate.

Remember, anything you donate needs to be in a fully resalable condition. Items should be clean and in good working order. That means no stains on the clothes or cushions, no missing buttons, no threadbare sheets. If you have textiles that aren't in a decent enough condition to sell, take them to a textile recycling bank instead, where they can be turned into insulation or made into new fabrics. You can also donate to charity through the clothing banks you see in supermarket car parks.

Look after your community

Think about your local community as well. There may be churches, baby groups and clubs that are in need of equipment or supplies. Alternatively, you only need to put up a post on Facebook saying, 'I've got four bags of baby clothes, does anyone want them?' Or, 'I've got an old Magimix... a toaster... a yoghurt maker...' There will always be someone who wants something for free and will be thrilled to take it off your hands.

Bra and beauty banks

If you have unwanted or unloved bras (in good condition) or if you have an abundance of beauty products that you no longer want to feel guilty about, bra banks and beauty and hygiene banks are brilliant initiatives to support. There are loads of fantastic campaigns around from charities like Breast Cancer Haven and grassroots movements like The Hygiene Bank, or look online to find a cause close to your heart or a local campaign.

My Favourite Places to Resell and Buy

Clothes

Re-fashion

This is the place to donate all your quality high street clothes. You pack them into a free donation bag and send them off. Your items are then listed online and sold and all the profits from sales are split between several sustainable charities. I love this site and use it all the time for my own clothes and for my clients, if they are willing to donate. I recently cleared out Candice Brathwaite's wardrobe and she has so many beautiful dresses she doesn't wear any more, which she kindly donated, and within 24 hours of them being up on the site they had all gone.

Re-fashion.co.uk

Timpanys and Vestiaire Collective

Timpanys is an independent reseller while Vestiaire is an international site for preloved designer fashion, but both are where I sell (and buy) high-end designer items. Perhaps you have a few pairs of designer shoes that you no longer wear but are in great condition? Sell them and put the money towards an upgrade so you can get something better – think of it like a swap.

The Timpanys and Vestiaire sites are also perfect for those dream items you want but can't – or aren't – willing to pay full price for. Maybe you want a handbag that costs £2,000 in the shops but if you spend time looking over preloved sites, you could get it for less. I'm constantly trawling these websites for things I want!

If you want to save the money and buy something for the best possible price, you should also refer back to The Saturday Test I spoke about in the Bedroom chapter (see page 30). Thinking and waiting will really help you reduce the amount of items in your wardrobe, and ensure it's filled with items you love.

timpanys.com
vestiairecollective.com

Clothes continued...

Wear Not, Want Not
It's great to shop local whenever you can. Katie Macaulay is an independent seller of preloved clothing on Instagram. I give her some of my clothes, buy some more, sell some more... Because she is local, I can take round a bag of clothes for her to sell and a couple of months later I get some money back so I can buy something else! Although most of the time it's more like a clothes exchange. I'll say, 'Have you got anything for me?' Then Katie will hand over some pieces that she knows will suit me. I've built up a relationship with Katie because she's close by, so investigate your own local area to see who you could sell to – and buy from.

Instagram @wearnot_wantnot

Amelie, Berkhamsted
Amelie is my go-to for capsule wardrobe items. I love to shop here. It's near my home too and has become my favourite boutique outside London. It's where I go when I need to bring something luxurious into circulation.

ameliefashion.co.uk

Shop local
It's more important than ever to shop local. Explore your area, ask for recommendations and support your local independent retailers.

Fashion and beyond

Bicester Village
This is my most favourite place in the world. You never leave there without a bargain! When I want to buy quality, luxury pieces to update my capsule wardrobe, this outlet shopping village is where I head for some amazing discounts. I bought my Jimmy Choo Hunter wellies at Bicester for £100, six years ago, and whenever I wear them people always comment. I have so many things I bought here and that I paid £200–300 for, instead of £1,000+. I normally buy shoes here, or blazers from The Kooples. But it's my ultimate shopping destination, because as well as buying high-quality fashion for less, if you are looking for new bed linen or pots and pans you can find bargains for the home here too.

tbvsc.com/bicester-village/en

eBay

It's the original auction site and eBay is where I source preloved – or sometimes brand new – items for less. I had been lusting after a pair of Givenchy studded ankle boots ever since they came out but I couldn't warrant spending £960 on them. So I watched and watched and waited and waited and got an alert on a pair that was £450... I still couldn't justify that amount of money but I had just got my book deal and Charley said, 'Just buy them.' So I made an offer... it was accepted... and they are mine now! They were still £350, which is a lot of money, but they were less than half price and I will have them forever. A classic investment boot.

eBay is also where you can sell your own items with minimal fees. The way I view the items in any wardrobe is that if you don't love something, you should get rid of it. And the easiest way to part with something is to think that someone else could love it and benefit from it. Trying to sell something is actually really hard work. I know that you don't always have time to take photos, list it, answer buyer queries, pack it and post it. You probably have bags of things that sit at the bottom of your stairs or in boxes in your spare room that you still haven't got round to listing. Although if you can get your niece or little brother to help out, you could pay them to do your listings for you.

For the amount of time it takes you, and the space those yet-to-be listed items take up in your home, I often think you're better off donating them. Unless it's something of high value, you will feel so much better once they are out of the house. One of the biggest reasons we hold onto things is because we just don't have time to action getting rid of them. But with any type of purchase you need to realize that the money has been spent. You're never going to get that money back. Once you realize this, you can let go and move on.

ebay.co.uk

Facebook Local

I also advise my clients to either try to sell or simply offer up items on their local Facebook page before they go anywhere else. You will be reaching people in your community who can come and pick things up, you won't have to pay for postage and I find that generally people look local to buy things first because it's quicker and easier. Big selling sites have become so large and we don't have the time to scroll through pages and pages of listings. Facebook Local is great for selling – and buying – smaller items of low to medium value.

Essential Kit

Tools of the trade

These are the pieces and places I turn to time and again because they really work and suit every home. This list forms the basis of everything I use in my daily life and job and how I organize when I'm decluttering other people's houses. Remember: don't go on a storage shopping spree at the start of the decluttering process or you may end up with more than you need. Get the essentials and as you add items back and can assess exactly what else you need, invest in any additional storage solutions the space requires.

What you buy really depends on your personal taste, how much space you have and how much you want to spend. Most importantly, you need to select the storage solutions that will help you create space. Here are some of my favourite items...

Baskets

Perfect for: every room in the house!
I use them: for scarves, shoes, bath products and countless other things...
Tip: baskets are brilliant for dividing up different types of product, just make sure your stuff doesn't spill out over the top.

Drawer Dividers

Perfect for: bedrooms, wardrobes, and bathrooms.
I use them: for underwear, leggings, sports tops, socks and small, soft items, but you could use them for make-up too (also see make-up organizer trays on page 187).
Tip: when you're dividing up different products, drawer dividers really help you to see what you have.

Dymo Label Maker

Perfect for: creating storage systems, particularly in kitchens, utility rooms and in spare spaces like lofts and garages.
I use this: for marking up storage containers.
Tip: Keep categories short and simple.

Kilner Jars

Perfect for: kitchens and utility rooms.
I use them: for decanting dry goods when overhauling kitchen cupboards.
Tip: Kilner jars will work with every aesthetic. I love them!

Lazy Susans

Perfect for: kitchens and utility rooms.
I use them: in fridges and cupboards.
Tip: the perfect solution to give you easy access to every item. I use them for everything from oils and vinegars to crafts and make-up.

Food Containers

Perfect for: cupboards, shelves, fridges and freezers.
I use them: to fill my fridge with structure.
Tip: plastic food containers are affordable, easy to clean and child-friendly. There are lots of eco-friendly options available too, so do your research.

Food Containers, Stackable

Perfect for: fridges and freezers.
I use them: to bring order to my freezer.
Tip: as above, plastic food containers are inexpensive, easy to clean and have a long life.

Large Lidded Storage Boxes

Perfect for: lofts and garages.
I use them: to organize items in large open spaces.
Tip: they're brilliant for keeping things clean and dry. Don't overload them and label them if you can.

Make-Up Organizer Trays

Perfect for: bedrooms and bathrooms.
I use them: to keep make-up and beauty products clean and organized.
Tip: they come in a range of sizes so you can find the perfect fit for your drawers.

Slimline Velvet Hangers

Perfect for: wardrobes, spare rooms and lofts.
I use them: for wardrobes/hanging rails.
Tip: wooden hangers are amazing, IF you have space, but slimline velvet hangers are my #1 tip – you can store five slimline hangers to one wooden hanger. You save so much space and it also dramatically improves the aesthetic of your wardrobe.

Other hero items

Heavy duty clothes rails
Rail protectors
Dust cover bags for handbags and fabrics

Favourite storage stores

Declutter Dollies Store

All my favourite items are listed in the Declutter Dollies Amazon shop:

amazon.co.uk/shop/dclutterdollies

iDesign

This is the site I go to for plastic containers for fridges and freezers, lazy Susans and make-up organizer trays. They stock some of my most-bought products.

idesignlivesimply.com

Wham World

Brilliant for plastic storage boxes for loft and garage organization.

whatmoreuk.com

Index

Note: page numbers in **bold**
refer to diagrams.

accessories 40, 45
airing cupboards 55, 86
artwork, children's 137

bags 40
Barbie™ 155
baskets 40, 54–5, 64, 86, 108–9,
   122, 125, 186
bathroom cabinets 49, 52–7
bathroom cleaners 85
bathrooms 47–57
   checklist for 57
   and cosmetics 49, 52–7
   medicine cabinets 56
   questions to ask about 51
   resetting 54
   spa-like 57
   storage for 54–5
   vision for 50, 54, 57
   windowsills 56
bedding 27, 87
bedrooms 23–45
   checklist for 44–5
   and clothing 30–45
   questions to ask about 27
   as sanctuaries 26–7
   and sleep quality 24, 26, 28–9
beds 42, 44
bills 126, 133
bipolar disorder 14–15, 181
bookshelves 107–8, 112–13, 116,
   141, 156
boundary-setting 138
bras 43, 182
Brathwaite, Candice 183
breakfast 75
'buying blind' 14, 53, 66, 77

calm environments 19, 64–5,
   117, 171–7

candles 100
cars 128, 173
CDs 113
children 145–57
   and artwork 137
   and bookshelves 156
   checklist for 157
   and clothing 148–9
   and decluttering 153
   and food waste 67
   and kitchens 62
   and medicines 56
   questions regarding their
      space 149
   and school things 156
   and screens 152
   spending time with 150–1, 157
   and storage 98, 108–9, 154–5,
      157, 162
   and toys 14, 108–9, 146–57, 162
chores 109, 173
Christmas presents 147
cleaning 84
cleaning products 67, 75, 84–5,
   88–9
clothes hangers 168, 187
clothing 30–45
   capsule wardrobes 31–2, 41,
      44, 184
   children's 148–9
   coats 122, 124, 168
   designer 183–5
   donating your 182
   and fast fashion 31, 32
   feel-good 32, 34–44
   fold 'n' roll 35, **36–9**, 41, 43
   letting go of 166
   packing 41
   quality 30–2, 183–4
   rental fashion 31, 33
   seasonal 34, 45
   second-hand 183–5
   selling 183–4

shopping for 20–1, 30–3
sleepwear 43
sock drawers 42
storage kit for 34, 45
and storage space 29
structuring 35
underwear 43, 182
clutter
   bathroom 52–3
   bedroom 28, 29, 32, 42
   and children 147, 153
   dining room 99, 101
   getting help with 180
   hallway 120–4, 127, 129
   kitchen 70–1, 77
   living room 104
   and mental health 20–1
   minimizing your 14
   office 132
   and relationships 28
coats 122, 124, 168
colour coding 35, 112, 127, 140
communities 182
containers 66–9, 77, 108–9, 186–7
cooking 75
cosmetics 29, 49, 52–7, 182, 187
cushions 109, 117
cutlery drawers 74, 97, 100

Declutter Dollies 11, 19, 187, 192
deep cleaning 84
depression 20
dermatologists 52
desks 135, 141–2, 164
dining spaces 91–101
   checklist for 101
   and feel-good food 96–7
   and home offices 133
   questions to ask about 94
   resetting 98
   storage maximization 98–100
dinnerware 75, 96–7, 99–101
Dolly Dash 17, 42–3, 56, 76, 88,

97, 100, 116, 128, 142, 156, 168
donation 168, 182
　books 113
　cleaning products 88
　clothing 32, 182
　food 68
　toys 153, 157
drawer dividers 34–5, 72, 186
drawers 35
DVDs 113

eBay 185
emotional attachment, to material
　possessions 20, 110, 137, 150–2
emptying spaces 35, 54, 72, 86,
　98, 140, 164–5
entrances 119–29
　checklist for 129
　and coats 122, 124
　and first impressions 122–4, 129
　and keys 122, 123, 126–7
　and paperwork 121–2, 126–7, 129
　questions to ask about 123
　and shoes 122, 124–5, 129
　size of 129
　storage for 122–3, 125, 129
　and under-stairs spaces 124, 129

Facebook Local 185
filing 140–1
first impressions 122–4, 129
flow 62–5, 73, 75, 77, 169
food
　containers for 187
　dates on 68
　feel-good 96–7
　preparation 75
　shopping for 14, 65–6
　waste 67–8, 72, 77, 82
fridges/freezers 68–9, 76
furniture, over-sized 165

garages 160–2, 165–7, 169
General Practitioners (GPs) 181

hand washes 52
hats 40
headspace, reclaiming your 20–1
heirlooms, upcycling 110

help, asking for 180–1
holidays 41
hotels 44, 85
houseplants 54, 71, 98

Ideal Home magazine 88
Ikea® Kallax units 108–9, 154
Instagram 19, 95, 101, 139, 177, 184
intimacy issues 28

jeans, rolling **36**, 43
junk mail 127, 129

keys 122–3, 126–7, 129
Kilner jars 66, 68, 77, 83,
　186
kitchen appliances 70–1, 77
kitchen islands 134
kitchens 59–77
　checklist for 77
　and containers 66–9, 77
　and counter clutter 70–1, 77
　cupboards 64–6, 73
　dining spaces in 92
　flow 62–5, 73, 75, 77
　and fridges/freezers 68–9, 76
　and grouping things 67
　how to organize 72–4
　questions to ask regarding 63
　resets 72
　and storage space 73, 75
　and throwing things away 74
　zoning 62, 73

labels 69, 186
laundry 28, 42, 75, 86–7
lazy Susans 69, 86–7, 186
Lego® 148
'less is more' mentality 14
living rooms 103–17
　checklist for 117
　laid-back 106–7
　questions to ask about
　　107
　random items in 106–7, 117
　scent 109
　special touches 117
　views 108–9, 117
lofts 51, 160–2, 165–7

L.O.L. Surprise! Dolls™ 155

magazines 116
material possessions, emotional
　attachment to 20, 110, 137,
　150–2
medicine cabinets 56
memory boxes 165, 166, 169
mental clutter 15
mental health 14–15, 20–1, 95,
　121, 133, 177, 180–1
'messy one, the' 50, 57
microwaves 71
MIND 181
minimalism 14, 26, 86
money saving 53
mood 108–9
mugs 100
multigenerational living 111, 176–7
music systems 71

nostalgia 110

office supplies 142
offices 131–43
　and boundary-setting 138
　checklist for 143
　in the dining room 101
　how to create 140–1
　'job spec' for 134–5
　questions to ask about 135
　resetting 140
　and sharing space 138–9
open-plan living 107
overbuying 14, 20–1, 44
　cleaning products 84
　cosmetics 52, 53
　food 65, 66, 77, 82
overwhelm 51, 126
overwork 133

packing 41
paperless, going 126, 136–7, 143
paperwork
　and bedrooms 28
　and entrances 121–2, 126–7, 129
　filing 140–1
　and kitchens 71, 77
　and living rooms 107

paperwork
    and offices 132–3, 135–43
parental guilt 150, 151
pasta 66, 67
pets 88
photographs 166–7
Pinterest 86
Playmobil® 155
Potter-Dixon, Lisa 29
professional help 124, 180–1

quality items 24, 26, 28–9, 30–2, 52, 147, 150, 183–4

random items 106–7, 117
receipts 136–7
records 114
recycling 17, 68, 87–8, 127
relationships 28, 133, 138–9, 143
resets 35, 54, 72, 86, 98, 140, 164–5
rooms
    fundamental questions for 16
    see also specific rooms
rubbish 17

sanctuaries 26–7
Saturday Test, The 30, 31
scarves 40
scent/fragrance, room 109
school things 156
screens 152
selling stuff 32, 183–5
sentimental things 166–7, 169
sharing space 138–9
shelves 98
    book 107–8, 112–13, 116, 141, 156
    floating 49, 98, 141
    open 107
    slimline 83, 89
shirts, folding **38–9**
shoes
    overbuying 20–1
    packing 41
    storage 33, 40, 122, 124–5, 129
shopaholics 20
shopping
    as addiction 21
    for clothing 20–1, 30–3
    for cosmetics 53

for food 14, 65–6
    local 184
skin care 52
sleep 24, 26, 28–9
sleepwear 43
sock drawers 42
sofas 109, 117
space
    creation 176–7
    reclaiming 14–21
    and wellbeing 14–15
spare spaces 159–69
    checklist for 169
    and grouping items 162–3, 169
    questions to ask about 163
    sense of purpose for 169
    and sentimental things 166–7
    and storage 160–3
    structuring 164–5
special touches 117
spices 76
stationery 142
storage 186–7
    accessories 40, 45
    bathroom 54–5
    and children 98, 108–9, 154–5, 157, 162
    clothing/bedroom 29, 34–5, 40, 45
    cosmetics 29
    dining space 98–100
    entrance 122–3, 125, 129
    kitchen 73, 75
    opportunities for 83
    shoes 33, 40, 122, 124–5, 129
    and spare spaces 160–3
streaming services 113
structure 35, 164–5, 175
suitcases 41
support 124, 180
Sylvanian Families® 155

T-shirts, folding **37**
television 105, 108
'Three Rs' 17, 32, 74, 129
towels 55, 57, 87
toys 14, 108–9, 146–57
    quality 150
    storage 154–5, 157, 162

Trail of Destruction 9, 24, 125, 160, 172
tumble dryers 86, 87
Tupperware 72, 76

under-stairs spaces 40, 124, 129
underwear 43, 182
unsubscribing 127, 129
untidiness 15, 50, 57
upcycling 110
utility rooms 79–89
    checklist for 89
    and cleaning products 84–5, 88–9
    inspiration for 86, 89
    and pet things 88
    questions to ask about 83
    and recycling 88
    resetting 86
    as store rooms 82, 89
    treating as a living space 82
    zoning 75, 82, 86

vision 50–1, 54, 57, 174–5

warranties 137, 143
washing machines 86, 87
washing up liquid 85
waste
    food 67–8, 72, 77, 82
    junk mail 127
wellbeing 14–15, 177
windowsills 56, 122
working from home 133–5, 138–43

yourself, being the best version of 31

zoning 62, 73, 75, 82, 86

Acknowledgements

I cannot quite believe I am even in a position to write these acknowledgements. This book was made for my Dollies who have been with me from day one, supporting me in all I do. They are the kindest, most loyal group of followers I could have wished for.

Charley, my Number 1. No one has and no one ever will love me more than you do. Thank you for being my constant. No matter what I ask of you, you are there by my side, sometimes moaning, but always supporting and loving me. I can't do any of this without you.

My baby girl, for allowing me the chance to grow my business by being dropped here, there and everywhere while I work late but yet always emerging with a smile – be it 6am in the morning when you get woken up to go next door so I can get to work before 9am, or 8pm at night when I collect you after working late. Rarely do I see anything but happiness exude from your beautiful face. I am the luckiest mummy in the world to have you.

Sacha, my muse, my sister-in-law, my confidante and the all-round funniest, kindest human I know. Your home is a constant source of content and your cafés have been my go-to home from home, keeping me fed and watered. Even if brownies and vegan chocolate cake are no good for my waistline, I remain committed to supporting you in making sure they are right for your customers. You are the sister I dreamed of.

Room, my best friend and the original marketing genius behind Declutter Dollies. Thank you for spending years (27 of them!) supporting every crazy decision I made, personally and in business, whilst I found my feet. Where would I be without you? From carpet coats to Ann Summers bullets in the cutlery drawer, there is nothing we have not been through together.

Helen, for coming into my life at the right time and being the funniest work partner in crime. You've supported me with so many of my jobs and sat with me in my freezing car for hours on the A41 as we beg it not to run out of charge on the journey home! You've been the perfect injection of friendship and work support I never knew I needed.

I have so many different friends and friendship groups, all of whom support me in so many ways. You all know who you are individually and how you have helped. I hope that I can return the support. (I probably have to be honest... there is definitely not a kitchen or room I am yet to help with!) You all know if I can, I will. Thank you for being you.

Alex Fullerton, for the hours you spent with me helping to write this book, making sure my terrible grammar was corrected and my words shone through as I intended.

The project team: Bess Daly, David Almond, StudioROY, Krissy Mallett, and Thomas Hedger for his amazing illustrations.

Last but by no means least, Steph Milner at DK for believing I had a message to write, and my management Carly Cook and Francesca Zampi at Found for finding me and nurturing and supporting my growth. I know I am a logistical, scatty nightmare. Who would have ever thought the organizer was the hardest person to organize!

Declutter Dollies

Dilly Carter is a professional organizer who works unwaveringly to help her social media following and private clients become more organized in their day-to-day lives, both physically and mentally. Declutter Dollies can help you declutter and organize your space, move you into your new home and plan your storage. Dilly also provides virtual consultations to provide you with support remotely.

For more tips and advice from the blog, or if you need help to organize your home or office space, visit *declutterdollies.com*

And why not become a fully fledged 'Dolly' and share your decluttering journey via Instagram @declutterdollies

General note:

• Always read the instructions of cleaning products carefully and use as advised by the manufacturer.

• Please check the current donation policies for your local organizations before making donations.